From Ponce de León
to Sir Walter Raleigh

ALSO BY JAMES F. HANCOCK

*From John Cabot to Henry Hudson:
Early European Arrivals in Northeastern
and Mid-Atlantic North America* (McFarland, 2025)

From Ponce de León to Sir Walter Raleigh

Early European Arrivals in Southeastern North America

JAMES F. HANCOCK

McFarland & Company, Inc., Publishers
Jefferson, North Carolina

ISBN (print) 978-1-4766-9578-5
ISBN (ebook) 978-1-4766-5473-7

LIBRARY OF CONGRESS CATALOGING DATA ARE AVAILABLE

© 2025 James F. Hancock. All rights reserved

No part of this book may be reproduced or transmitted in any form or by any means, electronic or mechanical, including photocopying or recording, or by any information storage and retrieval system, without permission in writing from the publisher.

Front cover image: colorized detail from a 1562 map titled "Americae sive qvartae orbis partis nova et exactissima descriptio," Lessing J. Rosenwald Collection (Library of Congress).

Printed in the United States of America

*McFarland & Company, Inc., Publishers
Box 611, Jefferson, North Carolina 28640
www.mcfarlandpub.com*

Table of Contents

Preface	1
Introduction: The Spanish Move into Eastern North America	5
One—Ponce de León's Ill-Fated Conquest of Florida: 1513–1521	13
Two—A New Andalucía, Legend of Chicora: 1521–1525	27
Three—The Epic Voyage of Giovanni da Verrazzano: 1524	38
Four—The Fiasco of Pánfilo de Narváez: 1527–1535	53
Five—The Bloody Campaign of Hernando de Soto: 1539–1543	67
Six—The Luna Colony and the Coosa: 1559–1561	83
Seven—Jean Ribault and the French Attempt to Settle Florida: 1562–1565	96
Eight—Pedro Menéndez de Avilés Takes Charge of Florida: 1565–1566	115
Nine—Pedro Menéndez Struggles to Control Florida: 1566–1572	128
Ten—Spanish Florida Staggers Toward the Seventeenth Century: 1567–1586	141
Eleven—The First English Intrusion into the Southeast: 1584–1587	151
Epilogue: Southern Atlantic America in the Seventeenth Century	169
Bibliography	177
Index	183

Preface

Most people know very little about the events that predated the Pilgrims' arrival at Plymouth. By 1620, however, the coast of Atlantic America had been extensively explored and charted by dozens of European sailors. Plymouth Bay itself had been visited on several occasions by Spanish, English, and French sailors. We know this because, in most cases, the explorers themselves published rich chronicles of their exploits. The Pilgrims even carried with them on the *Mayflower* a map of the coast of New England drawn by Captain John Smith.

The uncovering of Atlantic America started at its geological extremes—Newfoundland and Florida. The first explorer to reach Newfoundland was Venetian John Cabot in 1497, following the trails of European fishermen who had plied the Grand Banks for more than a century. The first to Florida was the Spaniard Juan Ponce de León in 1512, following in the wake of slave ships passing through the Florida Straits looking for fresh captives to labor in the mines and on the plantations of the Caribbean.

The story of the European unveiling of North America can be separated into two overlapping chronicles. The Spanish dominated in the South with only a few incursions from the French and English. The French, English, and later the Dutch dominated in the North with little Spanish interference. For this reason, I have described the precolonial period in two volumes—one covering events in Florida and the Southeast and the second dealing with activities from Chesapeake Bay to the North Atlantic. In these two books, stories are told about the explorations and aborted settlement attempts that occurred in the 110 years between Cabot's landing in Maritime Canada and the Plymouth Colony.

This first volume covers all the Spanish expeditions into southern Atlantic America and the Gulf Coast, including those led by Ponce de León, Hernando de Soto, Pánfilo de Narváez, Tristán de Luna, and

Preface

Pedro Menéndez. This book also details the early French and English attempts to settle in the Southeast that were considered by the Spanish as great infringements on their territory. These included the journeys of Giovanni da Verrazzano, Jean Ribault, René Goulaine de Laudonnière, and Sir Walter Raleigh. Verrazzano also made stops in New England, which could have gone into the companion book, *From John Cabot to Henry Hudson: Early European Arrivals in Northeastern and Mid-Atlantic North America*; however, since these stopovers were part of a single voyage that first landed in the South, I kept them here. I also included herein two brief excursions Menéndez sent to Chesapeake Bay from Florida.

In my accounts of the various expeditions, I rely heavily on eyewitness reports from the explorers themselves. Many of them published logs of their experiences, and whenever possible, these original narratives are used in my descriptions. To make these accounts more palatable to today's audiences, I have modernized the Elizabethan spelling of the English authors and have used later English translations of the original French and Spanish accounts.

A tricky issue in writing about the precolonial period is how to represent the thoughts and actions of the Indigenous people accurately. I have relied on histories written from a European perspective, as the First Nations did not leave their own written record. I have tried to produce as balanced an account as possible without glamorizing the actions of either side. To give as much background as possible on the Indigenous participants, I have added descriptions of their lifeways to the chapters that recount their first contact with the Europeans.

The European discovery of North America was often not pretty, as the Indigenous people struggled mightily to protect their cultures against the newcomers' onslaught. Interactions between the people of the two worlds generally started out friendly but soon deteriorated as the Europeans took food and land from the local populations by force. Hundreds of Indigenous people were abducted to serve as slaves and guides or were taken back to Europe as proof of discovery. European diseases would further decimate the local populations, emptying their land for colonial farms and weakening their ability to resist colonization.

My two books attempt to cover the full, complex story of the European discovery of North America with all its many fits and starts. I try hard to give appropriate weight to all of the French, English, and Spanish activities. The project started as a history of New England, but as

Preface

my research evolved, I found that I could not ignore Spanish-dominated Florida and the Southeast. It became clear to me that the Spanish played an extremely important role in the American colonial heritage, contrary to the emphasis often given to English activities in United States schools. A thorough discussion of the Spanish role in the settlement process also helps dispel "the Black Legend" first propagated in the sixteenth century that the Spaniards were more brutal and exploitative towards the Indigenous people than the English.

To enlighten me on southern events, I was pleased to discover the recent, well-researched, and engaging histories of Charles M. Hudson, Paul E. Hoffman, Eugene Lyon, Jerald T. Milanich, and John Worth. I also gained valuable insight from a number of earlier works including Woodbury Lowery's (1911) *The Spanish Settlements Within the Present Limits of the United States*, Carl O. Sauer's (1971) *Sixteenth Century North America*, and Margaret F. Pickett and Dwayne W. Pickett's (2011) *The European Struggle to Settle North America*.

Introduction
The Spanish Move into Eastern North America

The Spanish began their colonization of the Americas in 1492 when Columbus established a crude fort at La Navidad on the Caribbean island of Hispaniola. The fort at La Navidad was built when one of his ships, the *Santa María*, struck a bank and heeled over. After hearing from a local Taíno cacique, Guacanagarí, that there was much gold on the island, Columbus left the 36 crew of his wrecked vessel to build the settlement and search for gold. The ship was dismantled to provide the building materials.

When Columbus returned the following year, he found the fort burned to the ground, with no survivors. The original settlers had quarreled, individually taking as much gold and as many women as possible, and ultimately had been slaughtered by the local Taíno.

Columbus decided to establish a new settlement, La Isabela, east of La Navidad. He had brought 17 ships loaded with more than a thousand men—including soldiers, carpenters, stonemasons, priests, and nobles—and wheat seeds, sugarcane, pigs, horses, and guns. He introduced European crops and livestock "to acclimatize the European population to the new lands and open a space for the cultivation of cash crops intended for European consumption" (Paravisini-Gebert 2016, 11).

The Spanish found dense populations of Indigenous, agricultural people whom they saw as a source of labor they could easily exploit. "They were sent out to pan for gold on the islands, and they were expected to produce food for the colonists" (Hancock 2022).

Introduction

An etching of Columbus as he first arrived in the Americas; Theodor de Bry's America (University of Houston Libraries Special Collections).

The Caribbean Under Columbus

Columbus imposed a brutal tribute system on the local Taíno. He turned out to be a cruel and ineffective governor, and the Crown sent Francisco de Bobadilla in 1500 to investigate the situation in Hispaniola (Altman 2018). Bobadilla sent Columbus and his brothers back to Spain in chains, although he himself was drowned in a hurricane that destroyed his ship on the way back to Spain. While Columbus made many more voyages across the Atlantic over the next decade, his family was not allowed to exercise any authority on the islands. Ferdinand and Isabella sent Frey Nicolás de Ovando, a knight of the Order of Alcántara, to serve as royal governor. Ovando set off from Spain in February 1502 accompanied by 1,200 colonists.

Under Ovando, the entire island came under Spanish control

within a few years. Ovando defeated the strongest caciques and gave the Spanish colonists grants to use the Indigenous Taíno as labor, called *encomienda*, a system that had been initiated by Columbus. "The indigenous occupants were required to provide a tribute of anything the land proved to hold—gold, crops, foodstuffs, and animals, and they owed a portion of their time to work on plantations or in mines. In return, they were to be protected and converted to Christianity" (Hancock 2022).

The First Spanish Diaspora to America

By 1508, the gold found in the streams and mines of Hispaniola had largely disappeared, and the Taíno's forced labor was almost exhausted on the island. To find new wealth, the Spanish began radiating out from Hispaniola in several directions.

Juan Ponce de León was sent by Governor Frey Nicolás de Ovando with Juan de Esquivel to begin the occupation of Puerto Rico in 1508. Esquivel and Pánfilo de Narváez then landed in Jamaica in 1509.

> Diego Velázquez began the invasion of Cuba in 1511, joined by Narváez, who had left Jamaica, and Bartolomé de Las Casas, whose experience of the brutal occupation of Cuba would convince him of the immorality of the Spaniards' treatment of the Indians. In the same years, the Spaniards established a foothold in Panama and what they would call Tierra Firme (the northern coast of South America) [Altman 2018, 5].

Darién would become the first permanent settlement on the mainland of Panama in 1510.

Spaniards began flooding into the larger islands in what Altman (2018, 5) called "America's first gold rush." Gold was found in substantial amounts in Puerto Rico and in somewhat lesser quantities in Cuba. Jamaica was found to have little gold and, like the Bahamas and Lesser Antilles, held little interest to the colonizers.

To fulfill a deathbed promise made to his wife, Queen Isabella I, King Ferdinand II recalled Ovando to Spain in 1509 for an audit because of his treatment of the Indigenous people. Columbus's son Diego was appointed to be his successor as governor. Ovando lost his governorship but was allowed to keep the property that he brought back with him from the Americas.

As the Taíno workforce on the big islands became seriously

Introduction

depleted, King Ferdinand, now widowed and free from Isabella's control, ordered that the Taíno be gathered up from the other surrounding "worthless" islands to replenish their labor force. By 1513, these peaceful people had been almost totally removed by slavers, and the Taíno were well on the way to extinction.

From the Caribbean, the Spanish colonists then radiated towards the great landmasses surrounding the Caribbean. To the west, the Spanish moved towards the Yucatán Peninsula, Panama, and then Mexico. Hernán Cortés landed on the Yucatán Peninsula in 1519 and in 1521 captured the emperor, Cuauhtémoc, and the capital, Tenochtitlan, of the Aztec Empire (Hancock 2022). The Spanish would then campaign against the Maya of the Yucatán Peninsula and Guatemala, the Tarascan (Purépecha) of northwestern Michoacán, and the Chichimeca in northern Mexico.

The war of the Spanish against the mightiest empire in America—the Inca of the Peruvian highlands—began a little later in 1531 and was a much more protracted affair. It began when Francisco Pizarro at Tumbes led his army up the Andes Mountains to Cajamarca. There Atahualpa, the emperor of the Inca, was enjoying the hot springs and preparing a march to Cusco, his brother's kingdom. Pizarro, with his Andean allies, captured and deceitfully strangled the emperor after he paid a huge ransom in 1532, but the conquest of the Incas didn't end until the last Inca stronghold of Vilcabamba (1,500 meters northeast of Cusco) was conquered in 1572 (Hancock 2022). The Spanish invasion was greatly aided by a parallel civil war between the followers of Emperor Atahualpa and his brother Huáscar and the aid of several Indigenous nations that the Incas had historically repressed.

To the north of the Caribbean, slave traders forged a path through the Bahamas toward Atlantic America in the early fifteenth century. The first privately funded expedition was that of Ponce de León, who discovered Florida in 1513, almost two decades after Cabot's first voyage to Maritime Canada and more than 100 years after the first European cod fishermen had arrived in the North Atlantic. Sadly for Spain, Ponce de León and the North American explorers who followed him would not find great cities of glittering riches like Pizarro and Cortés. They would find instead a densely populated land of hunter-gatherers and farmers.

Introduction

Southeastern North America Before European Contact

When the Spanish began exploring Florida and southeastern North America, they found diverse cultures whose lifeways were strongly impacted by the surrounding environments. Most were part of the great Mississippian culture characterized by the construction of large earthwork mounds; mostly maize, bean, and squash agriculture; shell-tempered pottery; extensive trade routes; and centralized control with considerable social hierarchy (Blitz 2007; Hirst 2021).

Some of these societies, such as the Calusa and Ais of coastal Florida, were complex hunter-gatherers who did not practice agriculture. They were sedentary people and depended primarily on estuarine fish and shellfish for food. At the time of the Spanish arrival, the Calusa society had reached its cultural zenith and dominated most of southern Florida, collecting tribute from towns that were far distant from their coastal homeland.

Across the rest of the Southeast were agriculturalists, growing maize, beans, and squash. Most agriculture was undertaken in the rich soils and bottomlands along rivers and streams (Hurt 1987). Floodwaters deposited silt that enriched the soil and made continuous cultivation possible. This soil also held enough moisture that irrigation was not necessary. The land was cleared by burning, and fields were rotated. Maize seeds were planted in hills along with beans that would intertwine the maize as it matured; between the hills were planted squash and gourds.

The farming societies varied greatly in their mobility. Some, like the Roanoke on the Outer Banks of North Carolina, the Apalachee of the Florida panhandle, and the Coosa of central Georgia, lived in permanent, agricultural villages. Others, like the Cusabo of South Carolina, Timucua of north Florida, and Guale of Georgia, followed a residence pattern of seasonal migration. The Cusabo and Guale lived on the coast in the spring and summer and farmed, then migrated into the interior forest to hunt during the winter. The Timucua farmed in the interior during the early spring and summer and then moved to the cooler coast to fish and forage.

When the Spanish arrived, they were astonished at the number of Indigenous people they encountered. In southern Florida, there were 20,000 Calusa living in probably 50 villages (Marquardt 2004). The

Introduction

Apalachee in the panhandle numbered in excess of 50,000 (McEwan 2004). There were between 200,000 and 300,000 Timucua in northern Florida (Milanich 1996). When de Soto's men made their bloody march through Florida, Georgia, and Arkansas, they came upon an almost continuous series of farming communities representing many different tribal groups.

R. Douglas Hurt, in his *Indian Agriculture in America* (1987), suggests:

> When De Soto's expedition landed in 1539, the Spaniards found the Indians in the Apalachee region (modern Tallahassee) raising large quantities of corn, and one chronicler reported that the province of Moscozo was "cultivated with fields of Indian corn, beans, pumpkins and other vegetables, sufficient for the supply of a large army." Indian agriculture was so extensive near Ocala, Florida, that the Spaniards took a three-month supply of corn from the fields. Indeed, Indian agriculture and the Spanish appropriation of corn and other produce made the four-year De Soto expedition possible.... If the southern Indians had not been good farmers, De Soto's expedition would have perished or been forced to turn back because the Spaniards became dependent on Indian crops, particularly corn, for a major portion of their food supply [27–28].

A Great Dying

Within a few years of the Europeans' arrival, the vast populations of Indigenous people in the Southeast would be decimated by the introduction of European diseases to which they had little immunity. By the early 1700s, the Ais, Apalachee, Calusa, and Timucua of Florida were largely extinct. By the end of that century, all the chiefdoms observed by de Soto had collapsed, the mound-building societies had mostly disappeared, and the survivors had begun coalescing themselves into the historical groups of the eighteenth century, which included the Creeks, Choctaws, Chickasaw, Cherokees, and Catawba ("De Soto Trail: National historic trail study final report" 1990). In fact, at the end of the eighteenth century, most southeastern nations had little or no memory of the chiefdoms to which their ancestors belonged.

All across coastal North America would be a "great dying." Koch et al. (2019) estimated that there were probably 60 million people in the Americas before Columbus arrived in 1492, and by the 1600s, 56 million had died, a whopping 90 percent of the whole pre–Columbian

Introduction

Indigenous population. While war, starvation, and overwork killed many of these people, it was disease that killed the majority of them. This massive die-off would play a key role in the European conquest of North America.

ONE

Ponce de León's Ill-Fated Conquest of Florida
1513–1521

Setting the Stage: The Kings Designate

As is well told by John Worth in the preface of his book *Discovering Florida* (2014, xi):

> If there was a "ground zero" for the earliest European exploration of North America, it was the lower Gulf coastline of Florida. Long before Plymouth Rock, Jamestown, Roanoke, and even St. Augustine, the coast and bays of southwestern and western peninsular Florida witnessed a flurry of repeated Spanish visitation, including at least one expedition almost every decade after 1513. Even the founder of Florida's first successful settlement, Pedro Menéndez de Avilés, initially explored and fortified the lower Gulf coast within two years of his arrival.

Ponce de León was the first European explorer to land in the Atlantic mainland of North America. He was born in the small agricultural town of Santervás de Campos in the province of Valladolid in 1474 (Turner 2013). Nothing is known of his parents. As a young man, he apprenticed with a Spanish knight named Pedro Núñez de Guzmán in the military order of Calatrava. Ponce de León was with Guzmán during the Moor Wars in Spain and was present when the Kingdom of Granada fell in 1492, the same year that Columbus discovered America. At 19 years of age, Ponce sailed with the Spanish fleet to America on the second voyage of Columbus. Ponce participated in the wars against the native Taíno on Hispaniola and in 1505 commanded a company of Spanish soldiers that defeated the last independent Taíno province on the island, Higüey. As a reward, he was made governor of the province.

In 1505 Ponce heard that there was gold on the neighboring island of San Batista (today's Puerto Rico) and established a gold mining settlement there called Caparra, in the hills above what is now called San Juan Bay. He also established farms and cattle ranches to support his mining operation and was appointed governor of the island by King Ferdinand. Ponce grew very wealthy, but his bubble burst in 1509, when Diego Columbus, the son of Christopher, became governor of Hispaniola.

Diego Columbus removed Ponce de León as governor of Puerto Rico and in his place put conquistador Juan Cerón. When Spanish King Ferdinand got wind of what Columbus had done, he ordered that Ponce be reinstated and sent men to arrest Cerón and bring him back to Spain. Diego still had considerable clout, however, and in 1511 he ousted Ponce from the governorship once and for all. After giving so much ground to Ponce de León's rivals, King Ferdinand still wished to reward him for his loyal services, and he granted Ponce a patent to explore and settle the lands reputed to lie north of the Bahamas, a mythical place called "Beniny."

The King's Patent

The king's patent begins, as recorded by Frederick Davis (1935, 9):

Whereas you, Juan Ponce de León, send to entreat and beg as a favor from me that I grant you permission and authority to go to discover and settle the Islands of Beniny, under certain conditions which will hereafter be declared, therefore, in order to show you favor, I grant you permission and the authority so that you may go to discover and settle the island aforesaid, provided that it be not one of those already discovered, and under the conditions and as shall hereafter be set forth, as follows: Firstly, that, with the ships you wish to take at your own cost and expense you may go to discover, and you shall discover, the island aforesaid; and for it, you may have three years' time counted from the day on which this my patent shall be presented to you, or when the contract shall be made with you in regard to the settlement aforesaid, provided that you shall be obliged to go to discover within the first year of the three years aforesaid, and that ongoing you may touch at any islands and the mainland of the Ocean Sea, both discovered and to be discovered, provided they be not among the islands and mainland of the Ocean Sea belonging to the very serene king of Portugal, our very dear and very beloved son; and it is understood that you may not take or possess any profit or any other thing from them or any of them lying within the limits stipulated between us and him beyond only the things which should be necessary for your maintenance and provision of ships and men, by paying for them what they would be worth.

Ponce's First Voyage of Discovery

For details of Ponce's first voyage to Florida, historians generally rely on Antonio de Herrera's narrative titled *Historia general de los hechos de los castellanos en las Islas i Tierra Firme del Mar Oceano*, which appeared in 1601. It contains the only full account of Ponce de León's voyage and discovery of Florida, based on Herrera's access to original papers and court records, which are now lost. Herein, I use a translation of Antonio de Herrera published in 1935 by T.F. Davis ("History of Juan Ponce de León's Voyages to Florida: Source Records").

Ponce de León set sail with three ships and 200 men from Puerto Rico on March 4, 1513. The ships were the *San Cristobal*, *Santiago*, and *Santa Maria de la Consolación*. The chief pilot was Antón de Alaminos. After leaving Puerto Rico, they sailed northwest along the chain of the Bahamas, known then as the Lucayans. On March 27, 1513, Ponce's crew saw what they described as an island, which was likely their first sighting of the Florida coast (Turner 2013).

The fleet then continued to sail northwest in the open water until April 2, when they sighted what they thought was another island. Ponce named it "La Florida" because, according to Antonio de Herrera, "it had a very beautiful view of many woodlands, and it was level and uniform; and because, moreover, they discovered it in the time of the Feast of Flowers [Pascua Florida]" (Davis 1935, 18).

The following day Ponce went ashore to take possession of this new land. The precise location of this landing is not clear in Herrera's account, although it was likely in the vicinity of St. Augustine (Turner 2013). Herrera also gave no details on Ponce's activities or what he saw.

All three vessels then began to follow the seacoast and on April 20, according to Antonio de Herrera:

> they saw such a current that, although they had a strong wind, they could not go forward, but rather backward, and it seemed that they were going on well, and finally it was seen that the current was so great it was more powerful than the wind. The two vessels that found themselves nearest the land anchored, but the current was so strong that the cables twisted; and the third vessel, which was a brigantine, which was farther out to sea, could find no bottom, or did not know of the current, and it was drawn away from

land, and lost to their sight, though the day was clear with fair weather [Davis 1935, 18].

Despite these problems, Ponce was able to go ashore in Florida for the second time and, almost immediately, had a confrontation with the Indigenous people:

> Here Juan Ponce went ashore, was called by the Indians, who immediately tried to take the boat, the oars, and the arms.... [The Indians] struck a seaman in the head with a stick, from which he remained unconscious.... And they with their arrows and armed shafts—the points of sharpened bones and fish spines—wounded two Spaniards, while the Indians received little hurt [Davis 1935, 18].

Ponce regathered the Spaniards after the sharp fight and Antonio de Herrera tells us that "he set out from there to a stream where he took water and firewood and stayed awaiting the brigantine" (Davis 1935, 18). There the Spaniards encountered another group of 60 Indigenous people, fought with them, and took one captive. They then moved further down the coast after being rejoined by the *San Cristobal*.

The people who accosted Ponce and his crew were likely the Ais, who were much more aggressive and militant than the Taíno that the Spanish were used to in the Caribbean. It is likely that the Ais had already heard stories of Spanish brutality from Taíno who had fled to Florida. The Ais may also have already had confrontations with Spanish slave runners who were branching out from the Bahamas. The aggressive response of the Ais to the Spanish landings must have been a shock to Ponce, who expected them to either flee the coastline or cautiously offer to trade nonaggressively.

Ponce Rounds the Florida Keys and Finds More Trouble

On May 8, Ponce and crew rounded Cape Canaveral, which they called Cabo de Corrientes (Cape of Currents), and continued to the south, eventually reaching and rounding the Florida Keys, and then zigzagged northward, landing on May 23, in a bay on the west coast of Florida likely between Charlotte Harbor and Sanibel Island. There they collected water and firewood and careened the *San Cristobal* (Turner 2013):

ONE—Ponce de León's Ill-Fated Conquest of Florida

On June 3, Ponce and crew had a confrontation with another Indigenous people—the Calusa. As Antonio de Herrera tells it:

> And at this time Indians in canoes repaired there to reconnoiter the Spaniards for the first time. They saw that the Spaniards did not go ashore, although the Indians called to them when they raised an anchor to repair it and they thought that they were going away. They put to sea in their canoes and laid hold of the cable to carry away the ship; for which the bark was sent among them and, going ashore, they took four women and broke up two old canoes [Davis, 1935, 19].

Over the next few days, Ponce and his crew interacted several more times with the Calusa but much more peacefully. Herrera reported that the Spanish traded with them for hides and *guanín*, a low-grade form of gold made into body ornaments. Recent historians think that this gold was more likely collected from shipwrecks. Spanish ships had been sinking on the Florida coasts since the earliest days of discovery in the Americas (Allender 2018).

Regardless of its source, this gold interested Ponce greatly, and the Calusa told the Spanish that their cacique likely would be willing to trade more with them. Incredibly, they were told this tale by an Amerindian who spoke good Spanish. He must have migrated from Hispaniola or another island inhabited by the Spaniards.

Before Ponce could interact with this cacique, for no recorded reason, relations with the Calusa turned again ugly, with groups of them ambushing Spanish parties. In the largest confrontation on June 3, the Calusa made a major assault on the ships. According to Antonio de Herrera:

> There appeared at least twenty canoes, and some fastened together by twos. Some went to the anchors, others to the ships, and began to fight from their canoes. Not being able to raise the anchors they tried to cut the cables. An armed bark was sent against them and made them flee and abandon some canoes. The Spanish took five [canoes] and killed some Indians and four were captured [Davis 1935, 20].

One Spaniard was killed from two arrow wounds.

Two of the captives were sent by Ponce to the cacique to tell him that even though he had attacked his ship, he still wanted to make peace and trade with him. Quite frankly, Ponce did not want to lose the opportunity to find the source of their gold. The answer came back quickly, when a large group of canoes containing 80 men appeared and began attacking the ships, although the parties stayed out of range of each other. Antonio de Herrera describes:

> They fought from the morning until the night without hurt to the Spaniards, because the arrows did not reach them, while on account of the crossbows and artillery shots they dared not draw near, and in the end, the Indians retired [Davis 1935, 20].

Ponce Heads Home After His First Visit to Florida

After hanging around for another seven days, Ponce finally faced the reality that the cacique was not going to come to trade gold, and he decided it was time to head back to Puerto Rico. They departed on June 15 and six days later found a group of islands that Ponce named the "Tortugas" after the great number of turtles there. Antonio de Herrera writes:

> In one short time in the night they took, in one of these islands, one hundred and sixty tortoises, and might have taken many more if they had wanted them. They took also fourteen seals, and there were killed many pelicans and other birds that amounted to five thousand [Davis 1935, 21].

These islands, along with Florida itself, are the two principal geographic features that still have names assigned by Ponce during this voyage (Turner 2013).

The ships resumed sailing on June 24, heading southwest by west, and sighted another large island (probably Cuba) on June 26. They sailed along the coastline for a few days and observed canoes, dogs, and knife cuts in trees but no people.

Ponce's ships then sailed east, followed the Florida Keys, and crossed the Florida Straits to the Bahamas, where they arrived on July 18. Here, Ponce encountered a vessel piloted by Diego Miruelo, a slaver whom many credit with the first discovery of Florida when his vessel was driven there in a storm. Miruelo may have been sent in search of Ponce by the governor Diego Columbus to keep tabs on his expedition (Turner 2013).

After Cuba, Ponce was ready to turn homeward but still wanted to find the island of Beniny. While roaming through the Lucayan Islands in search, Ponce found an old Amerindian woman living alone on a lonely island. He took her aboard as a guide, and she directed them to an island she called Bahama, but they did not think it was Beniny.

While traveling through the Lucayan Islands, Ponce was buffeted by many storms and high seas.

In late August, Miruelo's vessel was lost in anchorage at a Lucayan Island named Guatao, but the crew was saved (Turner 2013). At this point, Ponce decided to split the expedition. Diego Miruelo and his crew were put on the *Santiago* and *Santa Maria de la Consolación*, while the *San Cristobal* was charged with continuing the search for Beniny. Ponce departed with *Santiago* and *Santa Maria de la Consolación* and returned to Puerto Rico, arriving some 21 days later, in mid–October.

The *San Cristobal* got to Puerto Rico on February 20, 1514, claiming to have found a large, well-wooded, and well-watered island that they thought might be Beniny. It is likely today's Andros Island (Davis 1935).

Thus, the first mission of Ponce came to an end without him knowing exactly what he had discovered. As Antonio de Herrera wrote in 1601:

> The discovery by Juan Ponce of La Florida ended without knowledge that it was the mainland, nor for some years thereafter was that assurance obtained [Davis 1935, 23].

Second Voyage of Ponce de León

After his voyage of 1513, Ponce de León sailed for Spain, where he was favorably received by King Ferdinand, who issued him a new patent to colonize Florida and Beniny. Ponce was told, however, that he must first subjugate the Caribs, the fierce nation inhabiting the Lesser Antilles. The patent stated (Davis 1935, 53–54):

> "Juan Ponce de León, for the expedition to colonize the island of Beniny and the island of Florida … to conduct at your cost and charge the vessels that you might wish." He was to do all in his power to convert the local people "into the knowledge of Our Catholic Faith and should obey and serve as they are bound to do … and if after the aforesaid they do not wish to obey what is contained in the said summons, you can make war and seize them and carry them away for slaves; but if they do obey, give them the best treatment you can and endeavor, as is stated, by all the means at your disposal, to convert them to Our Holy Catholic Faith."

From Ponce de León to Sir Walter Raleigh

Ponce did lead an expedition against the Caribs but was severely beaten. Mortified at this failure, he returned to Puerto Rico and for several years gave up the idea of colonizing Florida. While Ponce was in retirement, several slave runners had visited the west coast of Florida, and one of them, Pedro de Salazar, had taken 50 captives on what is now the Carolina coast between 1517 and 1518 (Chapter 2). These activities and the growing fame of Hernán Cortés in Mexico finally got to Ponce, and he decided to go back and take full possession of Florida under the authority of his patent of 1514. King Ferdinand had recently died, and he felt that he needed to swing into action while the getting was still good.

There is no official report or detailed account of Ponce de León's second voyage to Florida. The fullest account is contained in Gonzalo Fernández de Oviedo's (1478–1557) *Historia general y natural de las Indias*, which was published first in 1526. Oviedo was in the West Indies just after the second voyage of Ponce "and although a memory record," Davis tells us (1935, 58), "it has every appearance of being reasonable and authentic."

Oviedo's account of Ponce's second mission as translated by Davis (1935, 59) is brief:

> Not exhausted by his outlays and labors, he [Johan Ponce] fitted out anew with more care and at greater expense and equipped and put in order certain ships, so as to reach along the mainland on the shores lying to the North, that coast and point which projects into the sea about a hundred leagues in length and fifty in breadth [probably Charlotte Harbor]. And it seemed to him that in addition to what could be learned and known of the islands ... which are to be found there, also on the mainland could be learned other secrets and important things, and [that] those peoples could be converted to God ... as a good colonist, he took mares and heifers and swine and sheep and goats and all kinds of domestic animals (and) useful in the service of mankind: and also for the cultivation and tillage of the field[s] he was supplied with all [kinds of] seed, as if the business of colonization consisted of nothing more than to arrive and cultivate the land and pasture his livestock. But the temperature of the region was very unsuitable and different from what he had imagined, and the natives of the land [were] a very austere and very savage and belligerent and fierce ... when he disembarked, gave order, as a prudent man, that his men should rest: and when it seemed to him proper, he moved forward with his retinue and attacked by land and entered into a skirmish or battle with the Indians, as he was a valiant captain and was among the first, and not so adroit [in battle] in that land as on the islands, so many and such of the enemy charged, that his men and his courage did not suffice to withstand them. And finally, they

defeated him and killed a number of the Christians, and more than twice as many Indians died, and he escaped wounded grievously by an arrow; and he decided to go to the island of Cuba to be cured, if it were possible, and with a greater retinue and more strength to return to this conquest. And so he embarked and arrived at the island [and] at the port of Havana, where after he had arrived, he lived a short time: but he died as a Catholic and after having received the sacraments, and also died others who were wounded, and others of illnesses.

Ponce had completely underestimated the strength and resolve of the Calusa. Turner (2013, 31) puts it thus:

These were not Taino, whose culture Ponce grasped. He understood the Tainos. He had language skills and an established record of vanquishing them in arms.... The Calusas did not tolerate a settled Spanish presence in the heart of their territory. It would seem that besides suffering at the hands of Spanish slavers they had also been warned by other Indians [from the islands] about what Spanish colonial settlement meant.

While Ponce's second mission was a total failure, Davis (1935, 64) suggests:

This voyage produced a number of "firsts" of history for the North American continent: The first attempt to plant a bona-fide self-sustaining colony; the first effort to implant the Christian religion among the Indians; the first monks and priests assigned for permanent residence; and the first purposed agricultural, horticultural, and stock-raising enterprises.

The Myth of Ponce's Search for the Fountain of Youth

Today, many people associate Ponce's missions with a search for the Fountain of Youth. However, in his patent from King Ferdinand, specific instructions were given for subjugating the Indigenous people and divvying up any gold discovered, but there was nothing mentioned about a Fountain of Youth. In fact, Ponce never referred to the fountain in any of his known correspondence with Ferdinand. Ponce and the king may have known of rumors from the Caribbean Taíno that such a place existed, but Ponce was focused on locating an island that was filled with gold and slaves that he could make into a profitable new governorship. As Davis (1935, 25) suggests: "It is rather difficult to comprehend his expenditure of a large part of his fortune in an expedition just to verify their tradition." Martin Sandler (2008, 113) adds: "While he may have heard of the supposed Fountain of Youth, there is no hard evidence that Ponce de León was either motivated by or indeed searched for the fabled spring."

The story of Ponce and the Fountain of Youth was a fabrication of early historians that was perpetuated by those who followed them. In his account on the origin of the myth, Jesse Greenspan (2013) writes:

> Historians began linking Ponce de León with the fountain of youth not long after his death. In 1535 Gonzalo Fernández de Oviedo y Valdes accused Ponce de León of seeking the fountain of youth in order to cure his sexual impotence.... Hernando de Escalante Fontaneda, who lived with Indians in Florida for many years after surviving a shipwreck, also derided Ponce de León in his 1575 memoir, saying it was a cause for merriment that he sought the Fountain of Youth.

In Antonio de Herrera y Tordesillas's 1601 history of the West Indies, he briefly mentioned that the Fountain of Youth was of interest to Ponce.

Roger Chapman (2015, 92) suggests that "a cursory survey of US history textbooks on the treatment of Juan Ponce de León and the 'discovery' of Florida would suggest historical content is like an ice cube melting in the sun." The Fountain of Youth legend gained its first traction in the United States soon after the Spanish ceded Florida in 1819 (Greenspan 2013). The oldest city in North America, St. Augustine, placed a statue of the explorer in its central plaza in the early twentieth century, and the actual Fountain of Youth was claimed to be nearby. Even today, tens of thousands of visitors come to the site.

Lifeways of the Ais and Calusa

The Ais

The Ais or Ays lived along coastal Florida from Cape Canaveral south to the present-day Indian River (Ricky 1998; Davidson 2004). Their population size at the time of European contact was probably several thousand.

The Ais were mound builders. Their mounds consisted mostly of discarded shells from the enormous number of shellfish they consumed. Some were low, simple piles of shell structures, while others were mountainous man-made structures. One of their most impressive burial mounds at Fort Pierce is several hundred feet around in circumference and rises about 20 feet into the sky. A series of impressive stone steps lead to the top of it.

The Ais chiefdom was composed of several villages led by individual chiefs who were subordinate to a paramount chief. They were active scavengers of shipwrecks and took many sailors captive (Allender 2018).

The Ais were hunters and gatherers and did not farm. Shipwrecked sailor Jonathan Dickinson wrote in his journal of 1696 that the Ais "neither sow nor plant any manner of thing whatsoever" (Andrews and Andrews 1945, 36). The Ais subsisted on a wide range of native foods:

> They obtained their food from the fish, which they speared freely in the daytime and with the aid of torches at night, from oysters, clams, crabs, and crawfish, from the starch pith of the coontie root ... from aquatic plants and berries—the last named chiefly clusters of sea-grapes, prickly pears, coco plums (white and pink), and pigeon plums—and from the hearts and berries of the palmetto, all of which were eaten both fresh and dried [Andrews and Andrews 1945, 99].

For clothing, the Ais men wore a loincloth, described by Dickinson as

> being a piece of platwork of straws wrought of divers colors and of a triangular figure, with a belt of four fingers broad of the same wrought together, which goeth about the waist and the angle of the other having a thing to it, coming between the legs, and strings to the end of the belt; all three meeting together are fastened behind by a horsetail, or a bunch of silkgrass exactly resembling it, of a flaxen color, this being all of the apparel or covering that the men wear [Andrews and Andrews 1945, 23–24].

The Ais used dugout canoes that held up to 50 people. They were either poled or paddled. The canoes were made from a single conifer log by carving "a hollow trough or passenger compartment in its center using fire and stone tools" (Davidson 2004, 30). The largest of these canoes were seaworthy.

The weapons of Ais warriors were bows and arrows and throwing spears or javelins. The bowstrings were made of deer skin or entrails. They used the throwing spears to impale fish in tidal shallows during the day and at night in rivers from illuminated canoes. They also caught fish using fish weirs and cast nets of fiber.

They lived in huts built of saplings that were covered with thatched palmetto leaves.

> Ais villages consisted of a cluster of dome-shaped family huts. A larger central structure, usually the residence of the village chieftain served as a meeting place.... Ais homes were furnished with low wooden benches resting one foot off the ground. The benches were covered with reeds at night for sleeping [Davidson 2004, 33].

The Ais villages were not protected by palisades but were hidden from the eyes of Spanish slavers by extensive mangrove colonies between their villages and the sea.

The Calusa

The Calusa who battled Ponce de León so fiercely were a remarkably complex hunter-gather society that had reached its zenith at the time of his contact. They dominated almost all of southern Florida, collecting tribute from towns that were far distant from their coastal homeland.

When the Spanish arrived, there were probably 20,000 Calusa living in 50 villages. At their capital, Mound Key, they had constructed an expansive manor on top of a massive 30-foot-high shell mound that could hold two thousand people. Rituals were performed in a special temple with benches and a central altar, with walls covered with masks.

The Calusa built canals between the major coastal towns and inland waterways to facilitate movement and trade. Intricate weirs were built of rocks and shells to capture and store fish. They used a wide array of canoes, including seagoing vessels, small cargo carriers, and larger barges with platforms connecting two canoes.

The Calusa were a sedentary people and depended primarily on estuarine fish and shellfish for food (Ricky 1998). Hernando de Escalante Fontaneda, a Spanish castaway among the Calusa from 1549 to 1566, described all the Indigenous people of southern Florida as "great anglers [who] at no time lack fresh fish" (Reilly 1981, 396).

While they lacked agriculture, the Calusa had one of North America's most complex political societies. It was led by a paramount leader (or cacique), a war captain, and a head priest.

> A significant part of the paramount's authority rested on his ability to mediate between the secular and sacred realms.... The nobility, military, royal family, and other specialists extracted surplus from the commoners.... Outside the immediate Calusa domain, other polity chiefs paid tribute to the Calusa paramount, and each provided him a wife.... The

captain-general, or war captain, waged war on behalf of the Calusa [Marquardt 2004, 209–10].

In time of war, the paramount chief could mobilize a militia that was supplied with arms from all the towns under his control. All the leaders were close relatives of the king, and leadership was based on descent from the ancient founders of their society.

The Calusa were four inches taller than the Spanish (Marquardt 2004). The men allowed their hair to fall to their waists and wore only a leather breechcloth, while the women wore skirts that were woven from Spanish moss and palmetto leaves. The common people wore very few personal adornments.

The Calusa were outstanding craftsmen. Their art, with their carved and painted wooden masks, was "without known parallel in America" (Reilly 1981, 397). They produced an extensive inventory of skillfully made artifacts including awls, chisels, knives, hammers, scrapers, gouges, dippers, spoons, beads, pendants, picks, weights, and celt belts made from shells (Ricky 1998). Shells were used to make jewelry, tools, and other utensils. They used a shark's tooth knife to produce beautiful and sophisticated art, including tubs, bowls, mortars, pestles, amulets, and tablets. They produced some of the most renowned pieces of Amerindian artwork in the form of feline sculpture. They made technologically challenging, artistic pottery using imported clay for at least two thousand years and learned how to hammer and emboss the gold, silver, and copper from the numerous Spanish shipwrecks along the coast. They also used local fibers to produce excellent cordage, rope, and netting.

> In the Calusa religion, a sun deity was the universal creator and they believed that three supernatural beings ruled the universe. The most powerful deity was Toya, who governed the physical world, the second most powerful deity guided government leaders, while the third ruling deity influenced the outcome of battles, choosing the victor in advance.
>
> The Calusa thought that humans had three souls—the pupil of a person's eye, his shadow, and his reflection. The soul in the eye pupil remained with the body after death, while the other two souls left the body after death and entered into an animal. If a Calusa killed this animal, the soul would migrate to a lesser animal. Repeated killing of animals containing human souls would eventually reduce the third soul to non-existence [Thornton 2014].

Human sacrifice was a common practice (Worth, 1995). When the child of a cacique died, all households were required to bring one of their children to be sacrificed. When the cacique himself died, his servants were sacrificed to join him. Each year a Christian was sacrificed to appease the Calusa idols.

Two

A New Andalucía, Legend of Chicora
1521–1525

Setting the Stage: Pedro de Salazar Stumbles onto South Carolina

Spanish enthusiasm about La Florida was initially dampened by Ponce's violent experience. However, that mindset would be dramatically changed when the slave trader Pedro de Salazar and several others found their way to southeastern North America in 1517–18 (Hoffman 1979). Their reports of a docile and friendly Indigenous people and a verdant, rich landscape would spur Spain's interest in the land northward of what turned out to be the peninsula of Florida.

Little is known about Pedro de Salazar except that he was a slave trader who lived in Santo Domingo and was an encomendero with 50 Indigenous slaves (Hoffman 1980). He worked for Lucas Vázquez de Ayllón and several other important people in Hispaniola. Ayllón, a judge of the audiencia (Ferdinand's appeal court in Hispaniola), was very rich and powerful, having been granted over 300 acres of land and the labor of 200 local people. On his land, he established a sprawling sugar plantation.

The exact route and landing point of Salazar's voyage is not known, but he likely disembarked somewhere in South Carolina in what came to be referred to as "Chicora" or "the Island of Giants" (Hoffman 1984). The name Chicora probably came from the local people's name for themselves, Shakori. They were reported to be "giants" as they were much taller than the Caribbean Taíno that the Spanish had been exploiting.

Salazar's Foul Deed

The specific events that occurred during Salazar's mission are not known, but he apparently took captive as many as 500 local people, who had proven friendly. In later lawsuits concerning the disposition of the slaves brought back, a Pedro Romero

> testified that the Indians were very peaceful, had welcomed the Spanish with food, had taken them to their huts (bohios), and had shown a willingness to give whatever was asked of them. He also claimed that they seemed genuinely sad when the Spanish indicated they were about to leave [Hoffman 1980, 422].

There are also few details on Salazar's return voyage, but it is likely that two-thirds of the captives perished due to hunger. The Spanish were notorious for being inadequately provisioned. The surviving Shakori, upon landing, were tattooed and divided up among Ayllón and the other backers or given to the crew members as pay. Ayllón used his share as slave labor on his sugar plantation.

The slaves who were sold went for unusually high prices despite their weakness, perhaps because they were so tall and exotic-looking. The captives, however, proved to be bad bargains:

"The witnesses of the residencia all agree that the giants died soon after their arrival at Santo Domingo. In so doing they deprived some of the seamen of their reward; a dead Indian was worthless" (Hoffman 1980, 423).

Francisco Gordillo's Slaving Mission

In 1521, Ayllón sent Captain Francisco Gordillo back to the coastal area that Salazar had previously visited. His instructions were to find potential sites for colonization, and he was instructed not to bring back slaves.

Along the way at Great Abaco Island in the Bahamas, Captain Gordillo met up with Pedro de Quejo, another Spanish "slaver" who had a different sponsor, Ortiz de Urrutia. They sailed north together for about 350 miles, and when their soundings indicated they were near land they turned west and headed to shore. On June 24, 1521, the day of the feast of St. John the Baptist, they found land and anchored in a river that they named the Jordan River. There is some disagreement about which river this was, but it was most likely the Waccamaw River emptying into Winyah Bay just south of Myrtle Beach, South Carolina (Peck 2001).

Paul Quattlebaum, in his book *The Land Called Chicora* (1956), relates that the Shakori who first saw the Spaniards thought these newcomers to be "great sea monsters or gods." Their first reaction was to run to the woods, but two of them were overtaken by the Spaniards and dragged back to their ships. There they were dressed in Spanish clothing and given many presents. They were then allowed to return home, making the Spaniards appear to be friends.

Soon after landing, Gordillo held a ceremony to claim Chicora in the name of his sponsor, Lucas Vázquez de Ayllón. Quejo followed with his own ceremony that named the land for his sponsor, Ortiz de Urrutia. These two duplicate ceremonies would later become the subject of considerable litigation between Ayllón and Urrutia, with Ayllón eventually winning.

At this point, many small groups of Shakori began visiting the Spanish, who remained friendly and traded with them. Now completely trusting them, the Chicora chief sent 50 men to the ships to deliver gifts of skins, a few pearls, and a little silver. The chief also provided the Spaniards with guides to help cross the bay and explore the countryside.

Gordillo and Quejo stayed in the area for about a month, trading with the increasingly warm and friendly Shakori and exploring the land around them. In the latter part of June, the two pilots decided it was time to return to Santo Domingo, but before setting forth they blatantly betrayed the friendship of the Shakori. They tricked 150 on board the ships, offering entertainment, and then spirited them off to Hispaniola, in direct contradiction to Ayllón's orders (Johnson 1923).

Upon their return, Ayllón was enraged at the abductions but not too angry to accept some of the abductees as slaves. A case for their freedom was brought before a commission presided over by Governor Diego Columbus. The Shakori were ultimately ordered set free on the island of Hispaniola, where one of them was converted to the Catholic faith and baptized under the name of Francisco de Chicora.

Sadly, most of the Shakori captured by Quejo and Gordillo would not be as lucky as Francisco de Chicora. As Stone (2014, 201) relates:

> Despite the fact that the very legality of the Indians' capture was questioned, though not until 1526 after the majority of them were deceased, the other fifty-nine Indians were divided up amongst the financial supporters of the expedition and promptly put to work on the properties owned by

the various proprietors of the voyage.... Ayllón's share either were sent to labor on his new sugar ingenio near Azua or to his older mining holdings located close to Concepción de la Vega. Regardless of where the Indians found themselves following their arrival in Española [Hispaniola], nearly all of them died within a few months of starvation, disease, or general "mistreatment." In fact, only one of the captured Indians was known to be alive in 1526 and he was working in a pearl fishery in Cubagua. At the closure of the judicial proceedings in 1526 the Indians were ordered to be returned to their lands at the earliest convenience. Unfortunately, the rulings made little difference since the Indians, if they could be found, were likely dead after five years of laboring for the Spanish far from their native land.

Ayllón and Francisco Go to Spain to See the King

In spite of the controversy associated with the slaving, the returning sailors made glowing reports of the area around the Jordan River. "They described Chicora as a Utopian land that did not require military conquest and could easily become a new Andalucia when colonized" (Peck 2001, 184).

> Thus began the Chicora Legend, a legend that ultimately described the land of Chicora as a new Andalusia, a land abounding in timber, vines, native olive trees, Indians, pearls, and, at a distance inland, perhaps gold and silver. Flowing through this land was a great river, so wide and deep that it could be described as a "gulf" reaching deep into the land [Hoffman 1983, 419].

In the fall of 1521, Ayllón set about getting permission to found a colony at Chicora. He took Francisco with him to Spain to make the request, which was granted. While there, Francisco was interviewed by Gonzalo Fernández de Oviedo and Peter Martyr and made a great impression on both of them with his tales of Chicora.

Oviedo recounted in his *Historia general y natural de las Indias* (1526):

> In his country, the natives were white, ... the kings and queens were giants—elongated in their youth by rubbing their bodies with ointments concocted from strange herbs—then stretched like wax until they were of enormous height. He also told of a race of men in Chicora with marvelously long tails, that they bored holes through their seats through which the tails dangled when they were seated; that the people of Chicora made cheese from the milk of their women; that deer were kept in enclosures and sent out with shepherds [Johnson 1923, 341–42].

Peter Martyr reported in his *Decades of the New World* (1526):

[The Chicora] are governed by a king of gigantic size, called Datha, whose wife is as large as himself. They have five children. In place of horses, the king is carried on the shoulders of strong young men, who run with him to the different places he wishes to visit. ... I now come to a point which will appear incredible to your excellency. You already know that the ruler of this region is a tyrant of gigantic size. How does it happen that only he and his wife have attained this extraordinary size? No one of their subjects has explained this to me, but I have questioned the above-mentioned licencíate Ayllon, a serious and responsible man, who had his information from those who had shared with him the cost of the expedition. I likewise questioned the servant Francisco, to whom the neighbors had spoken. Neither nature nor birth has given these princes the advantage of size as a hereditary gift; they have acquired it by artifice. While they are still in their cradles and in charge of their nurses, experts in the matter are called, who by the application of certain herbs, soften their young bones. During a period of several days, they rub the limbs of the child with these herbs, until the bones become as soft as wax. They rapidly bend them in such wise that the infant is almost killed. Afterward they feed the nurse on foods of a special virtue. The child is wrapped in warm covers, and the nurse gives it her breast and revives it with her milk, thus gifting it with strengthening properties. After some days of rest, the lamentable task of stretching the bones is begun anew. Such is the explanation given by the servant, Francisco Chicora [Johnson 1923, 342].

Another Mission to Chicora

Ayllón signed the king's contract on June 21, 1523, and hired Pedro de Quejo to go back and explore Chicora more thoroughly for a settlement and to perhaps find a route to China. The expedition consisted of two caravels and 60 seamen and soldiers, evenly split. Quejo was given orders to search at least 640 nautical miles of the shoreline and generate a chart that future pilots could use to retrace his route. Quejo was also instructed to erect stone markers to signal the king and Ayllón's ownership of the land. In addition, he was told to capture a couple of locals who would serve as translators after being taught Spanish.

The first landfall of Quejo was on May 3, 1525, likely at the Savannah River, where he immediately snatched several locals. He then sailed north and, on May 9, located the mouth of the Jordan River (Waccamaw River), naming it Cape San Nicolas. There he was first attacked by the local people in response to the previous kidnappings, but they were placated by gifts of clothing and a promise that he would soon return the captives (Peck 2001).

After about a week at Chicora, Quejo continued down the coast of La Florida. In his travels, he first sailed south to Amelia Island and Fernandina Beach, and then turned and headed north to Winyah Bay, the site of his original landing in 1521.

> At first the Indians were hostile toward the kidnappers of their friends and relatives, but through interpreters [survivors from among the slaves captured in 1521], Quejo convinced the natives that this time they came in peace and that those taken in 1521 would soon be returned to their kin. He also made a liberal distribution of gifts—clothing is mentioned by Ayllón—which probably went as far as anything to calm the understandable anger of the Indians. Ayllón later claimed that Quejo had success with the Indians at least partly because he told them of the grandeur of Charles V, but that may be regarded as flattery. In addition, according to Ayllón, Quejo gave the Indians seeds for various Spanish plants that Ayllón hoped they would cultivate. The Spaniards even showed the Indians how they should grow them [Hoffman 1990, 53].

Quejo then continued as far as Chesapeake Bay, which he named the Bahia de Santa Maria. He returned home to Santo Domingo in July 1525, with a detailed chart of the coastline of South Carolina but, of course, no passage to China. This chart is now lost, but it must have been accurate, as Ayllón used it the next year to sail directly to Chicora and the Jordan River.

Tragic Settlement Attempt of Lucas Vázquez de Ayllón

Everything was now in place for Ayllón's colonization of Chicora. His intent was to peacefully live there among what he assumed would still be friendly locals, despite the history of Spanish kidnapping and slave trading. He would also bring on his voyage friars to spread the gospel among the locals.

His expedition was made up of six ships and around 600 people, including women, children, some African slaves, and a few priests. Francisco Chicora was included as an interpreter. For sustenance, Ayllón carried along cassava bread, maize, seeds for planting, cattle, pigs, sheep, and about 100 horses.

Two—A New Andalucía, Legend of Chicora

The settlers came largely from Spain, mostly the provinces of Badajoz and Toledo, and from the Indies: "men who had not succeeded in the conquests of Honduras, New Spain, and Tierra Firme (Panama and the coast of modern Colombia) or had grown restless once domination of the Indians had been achieved in those places.... Others left the declining economy of Spain" (Hoffman 1990, 60).

The spiritual contingent of the expedition was represented by Dominican friars Antonio de Montesinos and Antonio de Cervantes, and a lay brother named Louis.

The group departed for the mouth of the Jordan River in mid–July 1526 and arrived at Winyah Bay on August 9. However, disaster struck almost immediately, as the flagship *Capitana* hit a sandbar and disastrously sunk with all its cargo. Fortunately, the crew and Ayllón made it safely to land.

The location Ayllón selected for the settlement also proved to be a debacle, in no way matching the tales of Salazar, Gordillo, and Quejo (Peck 2001). Ayllón was forced to send out four search parties to find a better location with a good harbor, fertile soils, and friendly residents.

The various missions probed the area from Winyah Bay south to present-day St. Augustine or possibly as far as the Ponce de León Inlet. During one of these expeditions, Francisco Chicora deserted and made his way back through the forests to his own people. It is likely that when he had previously waxed so eloquently about his homeland, he was really plotting an escape should he be able to return.

Ayllón finally decided in early September to establish his settlement at a place he called San Miguel de Gualdape. Its location is debated but was probably along the Sapelo Sound on the Georgia coast. It is interesting to note that Ayllón did not select Port Royal Sound, South Carolina, a site that the Frenchman Jean Ribault would find desirable enough to build a settlement there in 1562. Ayllón either missed this spot or selected against it because it was sparsely populated. One of his requirements for settlement had been that his colony would be near a large Indigenous village (Peck 2001).

By the time Ayllón was ready to move, most of the settlers were already exhausted and on their last legs, having spent nearly a month in makeshift shelters. They had been continually soaked by rain; many were sick; and all were badly mosquito-bitten and, in general, miserable and discouraged. Regardless, Ayllón ordered the healthy men to ride to the new site on horseback while the rest traveled by ship. When the parties were reunited at Sapelo Sound, the fittest began immediately to construct houses, an all-important church, storehouses for food, and pens for the livestock.

The colony of San Miguel de Gualdape was formally established during the festival of Saint Michael on September 29, 1526. However, the rough-hewn town survived for less than three months, plagued by food shortages, unhealthy living conditions, physical exhaustion, and untreated diseases. Most of the supplies had gone down with the *Capitana*, and the colonists were unable to barter or coerce food from the local people. It was too late for planting, and they were forced to suffer through several unseasonable cold snaps where temperatures dropped dramatically from 70 degrees to near-freezing temperatures in a matter of hours.

Making matters even worse, Gualdape came under multiple attacks by the Guale, led by none other than their former slave interpreter, Chicora.

> It remains unclear from the documentation whether the Indian assaults were large, organized attacks on the actual settlement, or were more disparate harassments of smaller groups of Spaniards out hunting for food or mineral riches like pearls. Regardless of the size or shape of these indigenous strikes, it is clear that they led to many Spanish deaths and ultimately helped to bring about the abandonment of the settlement [Stone 2014, 203].

The final blow came on October 18, when Ayllón himself died, without a clear successor. Just before his death, he had designated his nephew, Juan Ramirez, as the new leader, but Ramirez was still in Puerto Rico. One of the soldiers, Captain Francisco Gómez, assumed overall command, but his leadership was weak, and the exhausted settlers soon broke into warring factions of disgruntled aristocrats.

Two major factions emerged, one led by Captain Francisco Gómez and the assigned leaders of San Miguel, and a renegade faction led by Gines Doncel, a minor noble from Santo Domingo. The renegades "soon obtained the upper hand," and Doncel arrested Gómez and the alcalde and locked them in his house.

> During this period of anarchy, a group of famished and desperate settlers attempted to move into a nearby Indian village and impose upon the natives for food. Garcilaso de la Vega reports the Indians soon tired of this and, after the settlers had feasted for several days, slew them all in a single night attack [Peck 2001, 194].

Gómez and his followers did finally regain control but decided it was time to abort the mission and return to the Antilles. The evacuation began in the latter part of October, with the last ship departing in mid–November. It was so cold by the time they left that seven men on the *Santa Catalina* died of exposure on the way home. Of the approximately 600 original settlers, only 150 survivors reached Hispaniola or Puerto Rico that winter.

And so ended the great scheme of Ayllón to settle Chicora.

> Ayllón left his family in straitened circumstances, as he had sunk his entire fortune in the Chicora venture. In order to recoup the fallen fortunes of the family his widow and his son, Lucas Vásquez Ayllón, attempted to secure an extension of the patent for themselves. The extension was granted to the son, but he failed in his attempt to recruit another colonizing expedition. The disappointment undermined his health, and he died in Española [Johnson 1923, 343].

Lifeways of the Shakori and Cusabo

The Shakori was one of several small nations that occupied the Piedmont region during the early colonization period. The low country of South Carolina was home to more than a dozen distinct groups of Indigenous people that have been grouped collectively together as the "Cusabo" (Waddell 1980). Some of the most important nations were the Escamacu (the largest and southernmost nation), called Orista by the Spanish; Hoya (a smaller nation, near the Escamacu); Touppa (Broad River); Mayon (Broad River); Stalame (Port Royal Island); and Kussah (north of Port Royal). These nations were distinct from the inland ones including the Catawba, Cherokee, Creek, Shawnee, and Chickasaw. All the tribal groups in the low country were probably able to communicate with one another, but it is likely they were multilingual people with many dialects. There is evidence that their language was related to the Arawakan of the Caribbean (Rudes 2004).

Few local writers bothered to record much about the customs of the Cusabo, although it is known that they followed a residence pattern of seasonal migrations, where they were located near the coast during the late spring and summer and moved as much as 80 miles inland during the rest of the year. Their total population size was probably around 1,200. Families lived in towns together in the summer, but in winter they scattered. The settlements in winter usually consisted of one or a few extended families.

Most summer towns were 10 to 20 miles inland, where the soil was better than on the coast. They had relatively large farms of corn, beans, squash, and melons but relied heavily on hunting deer, bear, elk, and wild turkey, fishing, and gathering nuts and berries. The work of planting and tilling was shared by everyone (Waddell 1980). They traveled by dugout canoes almost as much as on foot. Some of these canoes were large, carrying up to 10 men, and were seaworthy.

They hunted with bows and arrows, made of reed and pointed with sharp stones or fish bones. The Cusabo seldom planted enough corn to last them throughout the year and relied heavily in the autumn on the collection of black walnuts, hickory nuts, and acorns. They pressed the acorns for oil and ground nuts and acorns in a mortar and pestle into a paste to thicken their broths.

Their communities were, in general, small and autonomous. In the summer, a village might consist of a state house and 20 smaller structures where extended families lived. Each dwelling housed about 20 people. Their villages were usually surrounded by a palisade and consisted of several houses and a large council house for tribal meetings in which the entire community could gather. An area was often cleared around the council house where dances and games took place. The Cusabo played ball games.

The state house was large and could hold the entire community. The family homes were round with a domed roof of palmetto; the walls were of wattle and daub. The framework was tied together with bark rope. Each house had only one entrance.

A chief's function was essentially ceremonial, and it included presiding over tribal meetings and receiving visitors. Otherwise, chiefs lived like everyone else. The office of the chief was hereditary, generally passing on to his nephew on his wife's side, but women chiefs were not uncommon. The chief ruled with the aid of a council, which appointed a "war chief" who was awarded the post on merit.

Men wore loincloths made of deerskin, while women wore knee-length skirts of deerskin. Pants, leggings, and capes of animal hide were worn in the winter by men and women. Face and body painting was important for men, and designs varied in war and peace. Tattooing of the face and body was common in both sexes. They suffered greatly from mosquitoes and other biting insects, which they warded off with bear oil.

Two—A New Andalucía, Legend of Chicora

The South Carolina coastal people lived to a very advanced age. They practiced herbal medicine, with sassafras playing an important role. From the 1700–1701 journal of explorer John Lawson:

> You may find among them practitioners that have extraordinary skill and success in removing these morbific qualities which afflict them, not often going above one hundred yards from their abode for their remedies, some of their chiefess physicians commonly carrying their compliment of drugs continually about them, which are roots, barks, berries, nuts & c., that are strung upon a thread. So like a pomander (collection of aromatic substances to ward off disease), the physician wears them around his neck. An Indian hath been often found to heal an Englishman of a malady ... which the ablest of our English pretenders in America, after repeated applications, have deserted the patient as incurable [Waddell 1980, 54].

The Cusabo paid homage to the sun and moon and believed in an afterlife. They valued order and saw chaos as harmful or evil. They believed that the spirit and body were tightly linked, and one could not be healed without both being healed. Ritual healing was practiced by village priests.

Three

The Epic Voyage of Giovanni da Verrazzano
1524

Setting the Stage: The Continent Between

In June 1492, the Treaty of Tordesillas declared that all lands lying beyond the Atlantic Ocean, discovered or undiscovered, were to be shared between Spain and Portugal. Pope Alexander VI gave his approval in a papal bull. It divided the world into halves along a meridian 370 leagues west of the Cape Verde islands. All to the west of this line was to be Spain's, and all to the east was Portugal's. As William Bernstein (2008, 168) observed in his book *Splendid Exchange*, the power of these two nations was so great that "they could partition the entire planet like two schoolchildren swapping marbles at recess."

This treaty did not meet the approval of France or England, who were completely left out of the negotiations. They were even more offended when the Spanish decided that no other nation could trade with their American colonies, which were spreading throughout the Caribbean and the surrounding mainland. The English had a tiny toehold in Newfoundland, but the rest of the known New World was under Spanish control. The big question became—Was there other land available for colonization between Spanish-held La Florida and Newfoundland?

When Columbus arrived on the shores of what he called Hispaniola in 1492, the Europeans were clueless that a huge continent stood between them and China. Their knowledge of the geography of the world had come from the other direction from travelers who, like Marco Polo, had found their way to China going east across the Continent. The

Three—*The Epic Voyage of Giovanni da Verrazzano*

sea route of Vasco da Gama to India around the tip of Africa would not be discovered for another five years.

Of course, Columbus and the rest of the world were completely unaware that he had stumbled on the periphery of another continent and not the coast of China. That realization would slowly come over the next few decades. By 1525, the Spanish and Portuguese had covered most of the eastern coast of America from Florida to Patagonia, but the whole Atlantic coast of North America (except for Newfoundland) had not been explored. It was completely unknown how extensive that surface area might be, whether there was a passage to China through it, or if there were wealthy civilizations like the Aztecs and Incas on that continent. The northern Europeans were particularly keen to make these discoveries since the Spanish already had a firm grip on the southern part of the New World.

A largely forgotten explorer named Giovanni da Verrazzano would be the first to successfully navigate the whole Atlantic coast of North America and find it to be densely populated by a diversity of societies. Dozens of other explorers would come to navigate and explore North America in the future, but no one else would come close to revealing as much about the continent as Verrazzano. In a voyage of less than a year, he left us with a record that is breathtaking in its scope.

The Voyage Is Set

In 1523, a group of Italian merchants and bankers residing in France decided that the time was ripe to determine the extent of North America and search for a passage to China. They were particularly interested in obtaining silk, which could only be sourced in the Middle East after a long and costly journey across Eurasia from China along the Silk Road (Morison 1971). These bankers and other merchants formed a syndicate and obtained royal approval from King Francis. They chose the Florentine Giovanni da Verrazzano to lead the expedition (Wroth 1970).

The details of Verrazzano's life are sketchy, although he was likely born around 1485 in his family's castle, Castello Verrazzano, near Val di Greve, 30 miles south of Florence. When he reached maturity, he moved to Dieppe, France, to pursue a maritime career. There he made numerous voyages to the eastern Mediterranean and may have traveled

A 1768 drawing of Giovanni da Verrazzano by F. Allegrini (Wikimedia Commons).

to Newfoundland in 1508 with Captain Thomas Aubert on the ship *La Pensée*.

Remarkably, we have a written record of Verrazzano's enterprise in a short, 11-folio manuscript, discovered in 1909 and now known as the *Cèllere Codex*. This document is the report that Verrazzano wrote to Francis I upon his return from America. It is a pithy firsthand account

THREE—The Epic Voyage of Giovanni da Verrazzano

of the geology, plants, and people of North America that most historians consider to be mostly honest and accurate (Codignola 1999). For quotes, I use mostly the early English translation of J.G. Cogswell in 1841—*The Voyage of John da Verrazzano, along the Coast of North America, from Carolina to Newfoundland, A.D. 1524.*

Verrazzano Sails Off

Verrazzano was given four ships for the expedition, although two of them were shipwrecked shortly after departure, and a third was sent home with the booty from privateering along the Spanish coast. Only his flagship, *La Dauphine*, a 100-ton ship with a 50-man crew, made the crossing of the Atlantic. Accompanying Verrazzano was his brother Girolamo, a mapmaker, who prepared an ink-on-parchment world map for Pope Clement VII upon his return.

Verrazzano set out from Madeira, on January 17 and first touched land around March 1, at or near Cape Fear, North Carolina. From here he first sailed south toward Florida but soon turned to the north to avoid trouble with the Spanish, who were now active in the region. Traveling along the coast, he made his next landfall at what is now Cape Lookout, North Carolina. Here he had his first contact with the local people, who would later figure prominently in the settlement attempts of Sir Walter Raleigh in North Carolina.

As Verrazzano told it:

> We drew in with the land and sent a boat on shore. Many people who were seen coming to the seaside fled at our approach, but occasionally stopping, they looked back upon us with astonishment, and some were at length induced, by various friendly signs, to come to us. These showed the greatest delight on beholding us, wondering at our dress, countenances and complexion. They then showed us by signs where we could more conveniently secure our boat and offered us some of their provisions [Cogswell 1841, 42].

Verrazzano described the richness of the area surrounding Cape Fear, North Carolina, in almost idyllic terms:

> The whole shore is covered with fine sand, about fifteen feet thick, rising in the form of little hills about fifty paces broad. Ascending farther, we found several arms of the sea which make in through inlets, washing the shores on both sides as the coast runs. An outstretched country appears at a little distance, rising somewhat above the sandy shore in beautiful fields and

broad plains, covered with immense forests of trees, more or less dense, too various in colors, and too delightful and charming in appearance to be described. I do not believe that they are like the Hercynian forest or the rough wilds of Scythia and the northern regions full of vines and common trees but adorned with palms, laurels, cypresses, and other varieties unknown in Europe that send forth the sweetest fragrance to a great distance, but which we could not examine more closely for the reasons before given, and not on account of any difficulty in traversing the woods, which, on the contrary, are easily penetrated [Cogswell 1841, 42–43].

In the first European account of North American Indigenous people, he further described:

They go entirely naked, except that about the loins, they wear skins of small animals like martens fastened by a girdle of plaited grass, to which they tie, all around the body, the tails of other animals hanging down to the knees; all other parts of the body and the head are naked. Some wear garlands similar to birds' feathers. The complexion of these people is black, not much different from that of the Ethiopians; their hair is black and thick and not very long; it is worn tied back upon the head in the form of a little tail. In person, they are of good proportions, of middle stature, a little above our own, broad across the breast, strong in the arms, and well-formed in the legs and other parts of the body; the only exception to their good looks is that they have broad faces, but not all, however, as we saw many that had sharp ones, with large black eyes and a fixed expression. They are not very strong in body but acute in mind, active and swift of foot, as far as we could judge by observation. In these last two particulars, they resemble the people of the East, especially those most remote [Cogswell 1841, 42].

The first Indigenous people to interact with the French were likely the Algonquian Coree, who were living near Cape Lookout at the time of Verrazzano's arrival ("Native Americans of the South Outer Banks" 2015). All along the Outer Banks of North Carolina, Verrazzano would see and interact with a number of different Algonquian nations. One of these, the Roanoke, would be extensively studied and painted by John White in the first attempt to colonize Roanoke Island in 1585.

Pamlico Sound and Arcadia

After visiting North Carolina, the explorers continued north along the coast. Along the way, one of the sailors had a particularly harrowing experience but with a happy ending.

Three—The Epic Voyage of Giovanni da Verrazzano

While at anchor on this coast, there being no harbor to enter, we sent the boat on shore with twenty-five men to obtain water, but it was not possible to land without endangering the boat on account of the immense high surf thrown up by the sea, as it was an open roadstead. Many of the natives came to the beach, indicating by various friendly signs that we might trust ourselves on shore. One of their noble deeds of friendship deserves to be made known to your Majesty. A young sailor was attempting to swim ashore through the surf to carry them some knick-knacks, as little bells, looking glasses, and other like trifles; when he came near three or four of them, he tossed the things to them and turned about to get back to the boat, but he was thrown over by the waves, and so dashed by them that he lay as if he were dead upon the beach. When these people saw him in this situation, they ran and took him up by the head, legs, and arms and carried him to a distance from the surf; the young man, finding himself borne off in this way, uttered very loud shrieks in fear and dismay, while they answered as they could in their language, showing him that he had no cause for fear. Afterward, they laid him down at the foot of a little hill where they took off his shirt and trousers and examined him, expressing the greatest astonishment at the whiteness of his skin. Our sailors in the boat seeing a great fire made up, and their companion placed very near it, full of fear, as is usual in all cases of novelty, imagined that the natives were about to roast him for food. But as soon as he had recovered his strength after a short stay with them, showing by signs that he wished to return aboard, they hugged him with great affection and accompanied him to the shore, then leaving him, so that he might feel more secure, they withdrew to a little hill, from which they watched him until he was safe in the boat [Cogswell 1841, 43–44].

Verrazzano and crew continued on and discovered Pamlico Sound, which they were convinced was the entry to the Pacific Ocean. As described by Verrazzano:

We left this place from the day of arrival and found there an isthmus.... This is doubtless the one that goes around the tip of India, China, and Cathay. We sailed along this isthmus, hoping all the time to find some strait to the end of or real promontory where the land might end toward the north, and we could reach those blessed shores of Cathay [Wroth 1970, 54].

Thus, North America appeared to Verrazzano to be a rather long, narrow isthmus with a break in the middle. This mistake led subsequent mapmakers, starting with Girolamo, to show North America as almost completely divided in two, the two parts barely connected by a narrow piece of land on the east coast. It would take more than a century for this "Sea of Verrazzano" to disappear from maps and globes.

Further north, Verrazzano came to a place that he called Arcadia. This was probably Kitty Hawk, North Carolina. They were surprised that the climate was, in May, "somewhat" colder than Rome, the latter being on the same parallel—an observation that was to become familiar to northern explorers and settlers (Codignola 2019).

Here he anchored and went on shore and abducted a small boy.

> Going ashore with twenty men, we went back from the coast about two leagues and found that the people had fled and hid themselves in the woods for fear. By searching around, we discovered in the grass a very old woman and a young girl of about eighteen or twenty, who had concealed themselves for the same reason; the old woman carried two infants on her shoulders and behind her neck a little boy eight years of age; when we came up to them, they began to shriek and make signs to the men who had fled to the woods. We gave them a part of our provisions, which they accepted with delight, but the girl would not touch any; everything we offered to her was thrown down in great anger. We took the little boy from the old woman to carry with us to France and would have taken the girl also, who was very beautiful and very tall, but it was impossible because of the loud shrieks she uttered as we attempted to lead her away; having to pass some woods, and being far from the ship, we determined to leave her and take the boy only [Cogswell 1841, 44].

Verrazzano had undertaken what would become an all too common practice of European explorers, the abduction of Indigenous people—as a trophy of their exploration, to use as guides, or to be sold into slavery. The fate of this boy is unknown.

Sailing further north, Verrazzano missed the entrances to Chesapeake and Delaware Bays but discovered New York Harbor and anchored in the Narrows, now spanned by the Verrazzano Narrows bridge. He describes the bay and its people, the Lenni Lenape, in his report to King Francis I:

> We found the country on its banks well peopled, the inhabitants not differing much from the others, being dressed out with the feathers of birds of various colors. They came towards us with evident delight, raising loud shouts of admiration and showing us where we could most securely land with our boat. We passed up this river, about half a league, when we found it formed a most beautiful lake three leagues in circuit, upon which they were rowing thirty or more of their small boats, from one shore to the other, filled with multitudes who came to see us. All of a sudden, as is wont to happen to navigators, a violent contrary wind blew in from the sea and forced us to return to our ship, greatly regretting to leave this region which seemed so commodious and delightful and which we supposed must also

contain great riches, as the hills showed many indications of minerals [Cogswell 1841, 45–46].

Narragansett Bay and the Gulf of Maine

He continued his voyage east, discovering Block Island and reaching Narragansett Bay, probably near what is now Providence, Rhode Island. Verrazzano was likely one of the first Europeans the Indigenous people had ever seen, but they were not intimidated. Very soon after they landed, 20 long canoes surrounded the visitors, and two Narragansett sachems jumped aboard. The oldest one was a tall, long-haired man with multicolored jewelry dangling about his neck and ears, and the younger man was "as beautiful of stature and build as I can possibly describe" (Cogswell 1841, 46).

For 15 days Verrazzano and his crew were the Narragansett's honored guests, although they were careful to keep their women out of the sailors' contact.

As Verrazzano describes:

> We remained among them fifteen days to provide ourselves with many things of which we were in want, during which time they came every day to see our ship, bringing with them their wives, of whom they were very careful; for, although they came on board themselves, and remained a long while, they made their wives stay in the boats, nor could we ever get them on board by any entreaties or any presents we could make them. One of the two kings often came with his queen and many attendants to see us for his amusement, but he always stopped at a distance of about two hundred paces and sent a boat to inform us of his intended visit, saying they would come and see our ship–this was done for safety, and as soon as they had an answer from us they came off, and remained awhile to look around; but on hearing the annoying cries of the sailors, the king sent the queen, with her attendants, in a very light boat, to wait, near an island a quarter of a league distant from us, while he remained a long time on board, talking with us by signs, and expressing his fanciful notions about everything in the ship, and asking the use of all [Cogswell 1841, 47–48].

Much of the time was spent in friendly barter. The Europeans' steel and cloth did not interest the Narragansett, who "prized most highly the bells, azure crystals, and other toys to hang in their ears and about their necks" (Cogswell 1841, 47).

Verrazzano made many expeditions into the interior. As he describes:

> We often went five or six leagues into the interior and found the country as pleasant as is possible to conceive, adapted to the cultivation of every kind, whether of corn, wine, or oil; there are open plains twenty-five or thirty leagues in extent, entirely free from trees or other hindrances, and of so great fertility, that whatever is sown there will yield an excellent crop. On entering the woods, we observed that they might all be traversed by an army ever so numerous; the trees of which they were composed were oaks, cypresses, and others unknown in Europe. We found, also, apples, plums, filberts, and many other fruits, but all of a different kind from ours. The animals, which are in great numbers, as stags, deer, lynxes, and many other species, are taken by snares and by bows, the latter being their chief implement; their arrows are wrought with great beauty, and for the heads of them, they use emery, jasper, hard marble, and other sharp stones, in the place of iron. They also use the same kind of sharp stones in cutting down trees, and with them, they construct their boats of single logs, hollowed out with admirable skill and sufficiently commodious to contain ten or twelve persons; their oars are short, and broad at the end, and are managed in rowing by force of the arms alone, with perfect security, and as nimbly as they choose. We saw their dwellings, which are of a circular form, of about ten or twelve paces in circumference, made of logs split into halves, without any regularity of architecture, and covered with roofs of straw, nicely put on, which protect them from wind and rain. There is no doubt that they would build stately edifices if they had workmen as skillful as ours, for the whole sea coast abounds in shining stones, crystals, and alabaster, and for the same reason, it has ports and retreats for animals. They change their habitations from place to place as circumstances of situation and season may require; this is easily done, as they have only to take with them their mats, and they have other houses prepared at once [Cogswell 1841, 48–49].

Verrazzano also makes a number of observations about the lifestyle of the Narragansett:

> The father and the whole family dwell together in one house in great numbers; in some, we saw twenty-five or thirty persons. Their food is pulse, as with the other tribes, which is here better than elsewhere and more carefully cultivated; in the time of sowing, they are governed by the moon, the sprouting of grain, and many other ancient usages. They live by hunting and fishing, and they are long-lived. If they fall sick, they cure themselves without medicine, by the heat of the fire, and their death at last comes from extreme old age. We judge them to be very affectionate and charitable towards their relatives—making loud lamentations in their adversity and in their misery, calling to mind all their good fortune. At their departure out of life, their relations mutually join in weeping, mingled with singing, for a long while. This is all that we could learn from them [Cogswell 1841, 49].

Verrazzano Continues North

Verrazzano next followed the coast up to modern Maine, where he had much less pleasant interactions with the Indigenous people there, the Wabanaki, before passing southeastern Nova Scotia and Newfoundland on the way home to Dieppe.

As Verrazzano tells it:

> The shore stretched to the east and fifty leagues beyond more to the north, where we found a more elevated country, full of very thick woods of fir trees, cypresses, and the like, indicative of a cold climate. The people were entirely different from the others we had seen, whom we had found kind and gentle, but these were so rude and barbarous that we were unable by any signs we could make, to hold communication with them. They clothe themselves in the skins of bears, lynxes, seals, and other animals. Their food, as far as we could judge by several visits to their dwellings, is obtained by hunting and fishing, and certain fruits, which are a sort of root of spontaneous growth. They have no pulse, and we saw no signs of cultivation; the land appears sterile and unfit for growing fruit or grain of any kind. If we wished at any time to traffic with them, they came to the seashore and stood upon the rocks, from which they lowered down by a cord to our boats beneath whatever they had to barter, continually crying out to us, not to come nearer, and instantly demanding from us that which was to be given in exchange; they took from us only knives, fish hooks and sharpened steel. No regard was paid to our courtesies; when we had nothing left to exchange with them, the men at our departure made the most brutal signs of disdain and contempt possible. Against their will, we penetrated two or three leagues into the interior with twenty-five men; when we came to the shore, they shot at us with their arrows, raising the most horrible cries and afterwards fleeing to the woods. In this region, we found nothing extraordinary except vast forests and some metalliferous hills, as we infer from seeing that many of the people wore copper earrings [Cogswell 1841, 50].

Legacy of Verrazzano

Verrazzano's 1524 voyage was considered a failure by his contemporaries. The Northwest Passage to Cathay was not discovered or explored, although he thought that he had seen the Pacific Ocean at Pamlico Sound. As Verrazzano himself would describe his mission:

> My intention in this voyage was to reach Cathay, on the extreme coast of Asia, expecting, however, to find in the newly discovered land some such an obstacle, as they have proved to be, yet I did not doubt that I should

penetrate by some passage to the eastern ocean. It was the opinion of the ancients, that our oriental Indian Ocean is one and without any interposing land; Aristotle supports it by arguments founded on various probabilities; but it is contrary to that of the moderns and shown to be erroneous by experience; the country which has been discovered, and which was unknown to the ancients, is another world compared with that before known, being manifestly larger than our Europe, together with Africa and perhaps Asia, if we rightly estimate its extent [Cogswell 1841, 52].

In hindsight, his discoveries were in fact huge. As Codignola (1999, 32–33) describes:

Verrazzano was the first to report that the American continent was unexpectedly enormous, larger than Europe, Africa, or Asia. This was a discovery that, in fact, dispelled any hope of an easy way to the Indies. Furthermore, Verrazzano's description of the natural and human resources of the new land showed very little that could be of immediate interest to his financial sponsors in Lyon and Rouen or to the king of France.

The geographic information generated by Verrazzano had a significant influence on sixteenth-century cartography, but despite his great discoveries, Verrazzano's reputation never rose to the level of many other explorers of that era. His discoveries were made at about the same time that Hernán Cortés was conquering the Aztec Empire and Ferdinand Magellan's crew had completed the circumnavigation of the world. Verrazzano's reputation was even overshadowed in New York City by Henry Hudson, who was considered by most to be the discoverer of the city but, in fact, arrived 85 years after Verrazzano. It was only with great effort in the 1950s and 1960s that Verrazzano was given his rightful place as the European discoverer of the harbor, and the Narrows Bridge was named after him (Adler 2020).

Most scholars today consider his accomplishments to have been staggering. American anthropologist Bernard G. Hoffman (1961, 112) stated it thus:

He was the first to explore the gap between the Spanish ventures to the south and the English enterprises to the north; he was the first to establish the continental nature of [the Americas]; and he was the first commander to bring back anything resembling a detailed account of the natives of North America.

Verrazzano was to make two more voyages to the New World, with modest success. In 1527, he survived an attempted mutiny, reached Brazil, and filled his ship with brazilwood, from which his backers made good profit. In 1528 he again crossed the Atlantic, landing in Florida and then following the chain of the Lesser Antilles. Here, Verrazzano was killed by the local Caribs when he went ashore on one of the islands to trade.

Lifeways of the Coree, Lenni Lenape, and Narragansett

Coree

At the beginning of his journey, Verrazzano was the first European to encounter the Coree, whose North Carolina homeland was the meeting ground of three cultures—the Cashie, Colington, and Oak Island/White Oak tribes ("Native Americans of the South Outer Banks" 2015). The Cashie belonged to the Iroquois language family, while the Colington and the Oak Island/White Oak were part of the Algonquian family. It is not known to which culture and language family the Coree belonged; however, it is known that the Coree fought alongside both Algonquian and Iroquoian nations.

The Algonquian Colington were agriculturalists, organized in chiefdoms, in which a chief in a central village ruled the people living in several villages. While the crops matured, the people moved to seasonal villages to hunt and fish. As in other Algonquian nations, the chief ruled by consensus following the advice of a tribal council. The average Colington village contained 12 to 18 longhouses, with a population of roughly 120 to 200 people. Some communities were surrounded by a stockade, while others were not. The Colington Algonquians stored the bones of their dead in special buildings called ossuaries, after mass burial ceremonies. The Roanoke, whom the English later came in contact with on the Outer Banks of North Carolina, were of this tradition of nations.

The Cashie culture got its name from a special style of pottery they made. They had a mixed subsistence economy based on agriculture, hunting, gathering, and fishing. At the time of the European arrival, their villages may have been permanent. Their political system differed from the Colington nations in that each village was politically independent, although they were allied together. The Cashie also buried their dead in ossuaries but in small family ceremonies.

The White Oak/Oak Island culture has many of the same traits as the Colington. They lived in longhouses, exploited the estuarine environment, made shell-tempered pottery, and buried their dead in ossuaries.

Lenni Lenape

In New York Harbor, Verrazzano encountered the Lenni Lenape. The historical territory of these people included northwestern Delaware, New Jersey, New York, eastern Pennsylvania, New York City, western Long Island, and the lower Hudson Valley. There were two major groups of Lenape: the Nanticoke, who lived in western Delaware and eastern Maryland, and the Munsee, who lived to the north. There were variations in dialect, and although all Delawares probably could understand one another, there were significant differences in vocabulary and pronunciation between the most northerly and most southerly peoples (Weslager 1972).

The Lenni Lenape lived in mostly independent village units of families and clans along rivers and creeks. They were farmers and hunters, who lived in permanent, dense communities. Estimates vary widely, but there were well over 10,000 Lenape across their range and they lived in about 80 settlements around New York City (Burrows and Wallace 1999). Their villages had no set layout and were not palisaded. Their homes were randomly scattered set along the banks of a creek without any organization.

The Lenni Lenape had a matrilineal kinship system, where children belonged to their mother's clan and leadership passed through the maternal line. When they reached adulthood, men always married a woman from another clan and lived with their mother's family. The clan mothers controlled the land and houses and grew the crops, while clan fathers hunted for meat, cleared the fields, built the houses, and protected the clan. Within a marriage, men and women had separate but equal rights. Each village unit had a chief, but they had very little real authority. They were nominated by the old chiefs through heredity.

Men hunted most of the year when they were not actively clearing fields. From September to January and from June to July, they mainly hunted deer, and the rest of the year they harvested everything from bears and beavers to raccoons and foxes. They also harvested fish and shellfish from the bays of the area. In southern New Jersey, they harvested clams year-round. During the gathering seasons, women and

Three—The Epic Voyage of Giovanni da Verrazzano

children often accompanied the men, leaving the elderly behind. In the late fall, men moved to their hunting territories, where they remained most of the winter. Here they commonly built crude, temporary shelters or lean-tos of tree branches, but if they could find an overhanging rock ledge, they would use these for shelter year after year.

The men often worked together to hunt. One hundred or more men would stand in a line and beat thigh bones on their palms to chase deer to the river, where they were easily dispatched. They also lassoed deer and used fire to encircle and catch prey. They built fish weirs of stones laid across a stream in the shape of a V. Men would wade in the stream to drive the fish, and others would spear and net them. They used canoes made of hollowed-out logs.

Their villages had no set layout and were not palisaded. Bark huts were haphazardly strung along the banks of a creek, with no semblance of streets or a public square. There were three different-shaped huts, which the Indians called wigwams—round with a dome-shaped roof, oblong with an arched roof, and oblong with a ridge pole and pitched roof—but regardless of shape, each had a gaping hole in the roof that served as a chimney. There were no windows in any of the wigwams, only a single doorway curtained with animal skins. Within each dwelling, an open fire smoldered on the earthen floor, and the furniture consisted of tiered platforms of skin-covered tree limbs built along the walls to serve as seats and beds. Silo-shaped pits dug outside the wigwams were lined with straw and covered with bark; there corn, beans, and nuts were stored.

For recreation, they took sweat baths in small lodges built of stones and earth along creek beds. They smoked tobacco in clay or stone pipes for divination, to cure diseases, and for personal recreation. The Lenape had a game they called *pahsaheman*. In it, over a hundred players were grouped into gendered teams that would attempt to get a ball through the other team's goalpost. Men could not carry or pass the ball and had to use their feet, while women could carry, pass, or kick. Women could not be tackled, but men could attempt to dislodge the ball. Women were free to tackle the men.

Narragansett

In Rhode Island, Verrazzano encountered the Narragansett, who were a people of about 10,000 (Simmonds 1989). They were farmers who lived in large villages on the islands of Narragansett Bay. The Narragansett were expert canoeists and supplemented their diets with fish and other seafood. The Narragansett divided their nation into eight divisions, each ruled by a territorial chief, who was ruled over by a single sachem. They would become a dominant New England nation in the early 1600s when their isolation from the mainland protected them from the diseases brought on later by the Europeans.

They lived closely with nature and had a seasonal sustenance pattern. In the spring they caught many kinds of fish that migrated from the sea to freshwater rivers to deposit their eggs. In May they would plant their fields of corn, bean, and squash. Men helped clear the fields, but the women did most of the routine agricultural work, as well as picked strawberries and other wild fruit, and gathered clams, quahogs, oysters, and lobsters. The men hunted deer, beaver, fowl, and seabirds and also harvested clams and oysters from the bay. Men grew tobacco, which they smoked in clay pipes.

> Early tools were made from shells or soapstone that had been quarried from stone outcroppings on their lands.... The Narragansett also obtained wealth from the shores in the way of "Wampompeage" or wampum, as it came to be known to Europeans, harvesting the unlimited resources of shells from the bay and fashioning the pearl-like interiors of whelks and the purple shells of the Quahog into a currency that was used up and down the eastern seaboard. William Wood wrote in an early description that the Narragansett were "mint-masters," so skilled in their manufacturing that English attempts at producing counterfeit currency were dismal failures [Geake 2011, 13].

They built bark-covered wigwams near the fields. In the late summer, they harvested their crops and dried the corn and beans in the sun, then stored them in baskets, sometimes buried, for later consumption. In the fall and winter, whole families migrated into the interior forests, where they hunted deer, rabbits, squirrels, bears, and beavers for food and fur. Their winter home was a long house in which up to 20 families would live during the cold winter months.

Four

The Fiasco of Pánfilo de Narváez
1527–1535

Setting the Stage: Hope Springs Eternal

While Verrazzano was avoiding the Spanish and skirting up the entire Atlantic coast of North America, the Spanish themselves continued to focus their attention on La Florida. Still dreaming of finding great riches, despite the failures of Ponce de León and Lucas Vázquez de Ayllón, the proximity of their burgeoning colonies in the Caribbean gave them ready access to the Gulf and Atlantic Coasts of Florida.

The next Spanish expedition to North America was led by Pánfilo de Narváez in 1527. In a total fiasco, a mission that started with about 600 ended with only four being alive eight years later. The survivors endured an arduous journey by rafts across the Gulf Coast and then a long trek, naked and barefoot, across the American Southwest to Mexico City. The enormity of Narváez's failure set back Spanish interest in Florida for decades. "Narváez has gone down in history as one of the most ruthless yet incompetent conquistadors of the colonial era" (Minster 2019).

The expedition of Narváez is well documented in two publications that will be heavily referenced here. One is by the survivor Álvar Núñez Cabeza de Vaca in his 1542 *La relación y comentarios* (The Account and Commentaries), which was retitled *Naufragios y comentarios* (Shipwrecks and Commentaries) in later editions. I quote from Bandelier's 1905 translation: *The Journey of Alvar Nuñez Cabeza de Vaca and His Companions from Florida to the Pacific, 1528–1536.*

The second important source is Gonzalo Fernández de Oviedo's

Historia general y natural de las Indias (1526). Most of Oviedo's account came from an official report received from the Narváez survivors in 1539 by the Real Audiencia of Santo Domingo, but its last chapter was based on the first edition of Cabeza de Vaca's *La relación y comentarios* and interviews with the author at the royal court. I quote from Davenport's 1923 translation: *The Expedition of Pánfilo de Narváez* by Gonzalo Fernández Oviedo Y Valdes.

Who Was Pánfilo de Narváez?

Narváez was born in Valladolid, Spain, in about 1478. He entered military service as a youth and was involved in the Spanish conquest of Jamaica in 1509. Two years later, he commanded a company of archers during Diego Velázquez de Cuéllar's conquest of Cuba. There he presided over the terrible massacre of Caonao, where 500 defenseless Amerindians huddled together in a large house were put to the sword. Regardless, he was rewarded for his services with public offices and extensive land grants on the island.

In 1520, Pánfilo was sent to Mexico by Diego Velázquez, then the governor of Cuba, to take over the invasion of Mexico from Hernán Cortés. Cortés had to leave Tenochtitlan to meet Pánfilo's forces on the coast, and even though Pánfilo's soldiers outnumbered those of Cortés three to one, Pánfilo was defeated in the battle of Cempoala and spent two years in the garrison of Veracruz before being released to Spain. Once home, he was made an adelantado by King Charles V, with the right to explore and colonize La Florida.

The Expedition of Pánfilo de Narváez

Pánfilo de Narváez departed from Sanlúcar de Barrameda in southern Spain on June 7, 1527, with five ships and 700 men. He arrived at Santo Domingo (Hispaniola) in August, where he remained for 40 days. During that time more than 100 of his men deserted, likely in response to word of Lucas Vázquez de Ayllón's failed mission in which 450 of 600 men had perished.

In September, Narváez went to Santiago de Cuba, where he was hit by a hurricane that sank two of his ships, killing 50 men and several

Four—The Fiasco of Pánfilo de Narváez

horses. He remained in Cuba until late February 1528 and then put to sea in four boats with 400 men and 80 horses. After battling more storms and strong currents for more than a month, they spotted land in Florida and stumbled into Boca Ciega Bay, north of the entrance to Tampa Bay. Here they found an abandoned village.

> On the following day, Good Friday, they landed with as many of the men as they could take in the small boats. They disembarked close to the huts. They found no people in the huts because they had been abandoned. One of the huts was so large that three hundred people could crowd into it. The other huts were small. They found many fish nets, and in one of the huts, they found a golden timbrel [Davenport 1923, 129].

The governor ordered flags to be raised in honor of His Majesty and took possession of the land. As Oviedo describes:

> The following day, Easter Sunday, the Indians of that town came and talked to the Christians, but they could not make themselves understood. It seemed as if they were threatening them and telling them to leave the land. They made gestures and fierce threats. Having done this, they left [Davenport 1923, 130].

The Narváez expedition had made their first contact with a group representing the Tocobaga of the Safety Harbor culture, whose range extended along the central Gulf Coast of Florida.

The following day Narváez and 40 soldiers began exploring the shores of Tampa Bay. About 15 miles from where they had landed, they found some more Tocobaga people, captured four, and then questioned them about where they could find maize. They were guided to a village with a small field, where they also found Spanish freight boxes being used as coffins. These Narváez ordered burned. They also found shoes, pieces of linen and woven cloth, and some iron. They asked the Tocobaga where they got them, and they indicated by signs that they had come from shipwrecks.

The Spaniards then showed them some gold, and the local people indicated that there was none here, but if they traveled northward to a place called Apalachee, they would find a good deal of it, along with a great quantity of maize. This excited the Spanish, and they continued their journey, taking a number of Tocobaga with them. After traveling another 30 miles or so, they found another small village with 12 or 15 houses and a little maize. They rested there for two days but did not see a single person before deciding to return to their base camp.

Narváez Divides His Forces

On May 1, 1528, Narváez decided to split the expedition into two contingents, one traveling by land and the other by sea. An army of 300 would march overland to the north, and another 100 would travel by sea up the coast and meet them later. He was convinced that the mouth of Tampa Bay was to the north when, in fact, it was south of him. He asked the others what they thought of his plan, and Álvar Núñez Cabeza de Vaca, who was treasurer of the expedition and second-in-command, declared that he was strongly opposed. In his words:

> I replied that it seemed to me in no manner advisable to forsake the ships until they were in a safe port, held and occupied by us. I told him to consider that the pilots were at a loss, disagreeing among themselves, undecided as to what course to pursue. Moreover, the horses would not be with us in case we needed them, and, furthermore, we had no interpreter to make ourselves understood by the natives; hence we could have no parley with them. Neither did we know what to expect from the land we were entering, having no knowledge of what it was, what it might contain and by what kind of people it was inhabited, nor in what part of it we were; finally, we had not the supplies required for penetrating into an unknown country, for of the stores left in the ships not more than one pound of biscuit and one of bacon could be given as rations to each man for the journey, so that, in my opinion, we should re-embark and sail in quest of land and harbor better adapted to settlement, since the country which we had seen was the most deserted and the poorest ever found in those parts [Bandelier 1905, 14–15].

Cabeza de Vaca was outvoted by the rest of the leadership, and Narváez ordered the men to get ready to go. He also made a plea to Cabeza de Vaca to take charge of the ships. As Cabeza de Vaca tells it:

> After the meeting was over he [Narváez], on that same evening, saying that it seemed to him as if he could not trust anybody, sent me word that he begged me to take charge of that part of the expedition, and as, in spite of his insistency, I declined, he asked for the reasons of my refusal, I then told him that I refused to accept because I felt sure he would never see the ships again, or be seen by their crews anymore; that, seeing how utterly unprepared he was for moving inland, I preferred to share the risk with him and his people, and suffer what they would have to suffer, rather than take charge of the vessels and thus give occasion for saying that I opposed the journey and remained out of fear, which would place my honor in jeopardy. So that I would much rather expose of my life than, under these circumstances, my good name [Bandelier 1905, 17–18].

Four—The Fiasco of Pánfilo de Narváez

The ships were put under the command of one of Narváez's lieutenants named Caravallo. Narváez then headed off across the land with 40 mounted men and 260 on foot.

> They traveled inland for fifteen days, with [only] a pound of bread and a half ration of salt pork [to the man] until they arrived at a river which they swam [the Withlacoochee]. After they had crossed the river they were attacked by two hundred Indians. They captured five or six Indians. The Indians took them to their houses which were close by. They found a great deal of corn in the field, which was ready to be eaten [Davenport 1923, 132].

At this point, the soldiers implored Narváez to send exploratory parties downstream to find the ships, but the eventual search was in vain. In fact, they would never see the ships again. Just as Cabeza de Vaca had warned, Caravallo was unable to find the harbor to the north, and after turning around and locating it about 15 miles to the south, he was then unable to find Narváez. He cruised up and down the coast for nearly a year before finally giving up and going to Mexico.

Narváez Continues North

Having no alternative, Narváez ordered the party to continue north. The locals had told them that they could find plenty of gold and a land of riches if they traveled a short distance north to the empire of the Apalachee. The locals likely fabricated this story to get them to leave.

The trip to Apalachee wound up taking nearly six weeks, covering about 250 miles, and ended on the shores of Lake Miccosukee near the present Georgia border. As described by Cartwright (1998, 27):

> The soldiers were expecting golden temples and possibly casks of wine and legs of mutton. What they found were forty thatched huts and a small store of corn and deerskins. A few wretched women and children huddled near a campfire, but the men had vanished into the forest. The Spaniards were bitterly disappointed and near exhaustion. Their faces and arms were ripped by thorns and infected from insect bites, and their bodies blistered under their heavy shirts of mail. Scouting parties reported that beyond this village, the country was barely passable, with nothing but lakes, marshes, fallen trees, tangles of underbrush, and hostile Indians.

For the next month, the harried Spaniards stayed in Apalachee trying to recover their energy, but they had little opportunity to rest. As Oviedo relates:

> After the Spanish had been there two days, the Indians and their cacique came to them in a peaceful manner and asked that their women and children be returned to them. Narváez complied but kept the cacique captive. The following day, 200 Indians attacked them and set the huts on fire where the Christians were staying. The Spanish fought them off and they retired to the woods. No Indians were captured, but two or three were killed. The Spanish could capture no Indians, but they killed two or three of them. The following day another two hundred Indians attacked and were again repulsed [Davenport 1923, 135].

After depleting the food supply at Apalachee, Narváez concluded that they had to continue their journey and try to find their ships. It was clear that the group had further hard times ahead of them as they had made several forages into the surrounding area and found few people.

> They asked the cacique about the country further on, and they were told there were fewer people and less to eat than where they were, until about eight days' journey from there, there was a town called Aute with a great deal of maize and beans, that was near the sea [Davenport 1923, 135].

This march proved to be even worse than the last. As Cartwright (1998, 27) vividly describes:

> A merciless July sun turned the woods into a furnace, and the bone-tired and dispirited conquistadors stumbled like zombies through lashing branches and putrid bogs, conquering nothing, not even the terror in their own hearts. They crossed creeks in which alligators were indistinguishable from clumps of green scum, hauling their sore bodies over fallen tree trunks as wide as barrels. Flies swarmed over their bleeding, sweating faces, while ticks and redbugs crawled beneath the blistering metal of their armor and made nests. Each step brought them palpably closer to death. As the Spaniards were attempting to ford a lake, a band of large, naked Indians attacked. Arrows pierced their armor as though it were goose down, wounding a number of the men, including Cabeza de Vaca.

After several days of such miserable travel, the expedition reached the mouth of the Ochlockonee River, where, to no one's surprise, there were no ships awaiting them. At this point, Cabeza de Vaca decided that their only hope was to build some boats and escape by the sea. This would be an incredible challenge, as Oviedo relates:

> We had no tools, iron, forge, oakum, pitch, rigging, or any of the many things needed for it, and we especially lacked someone to provide expertise. Worst of all, there would be nothing to eat while the vessels were being built nor skilled men to do the job [Bandelier 1905, 37].

Four—The Fiasco of Pánfilo de Narváez

At least one-third of the men were too sick to work, and every day, the number of able men decreased. They slaughtered most of their remaining horses to provide some sustenance. Parties sent out to forage were ambushed and killed by roving bands of Amerindians.

Remarkably, with great ingenuity, they managed to construct five barges by working steadily from August 4 to September 20. As Cabeza de Vaca describes:

> Each one measured twenty-two cubits and was caulked with the palmetto fibers. We caulked them with a kind of pitch from resin made by a Greek named Don Theodoro from some pine trees and the palmetto fiber. From the horses' tails and manes, we made rope and rigging; out of our shirts, we made sails; and from some junipers near there, we made oars, which we thought were necessary. And that land to which we had been brought by our sins was such that it was very difficult to find stones for ballast and anchors. Nowhere in it had we seen any. We skinned the legs of the horses in one piece and cured the hides to make skins for carrying water [Bandelier 1905, 38–39].

They set sail on September 22, 1528, with 242 survivors packed in the five ships, and followed the Gulf Coast west. Suffering frequent storms, great hunger, and much thirst, about 80 survivors, including Cabeza de Vaca, finally landed in a hurricane on the western shore of a barrier island, either Galveston or Follet's Island. Most of the other soldiers were lost in the storm, including Pánfilo de Narváez.

Soon after landing, the party was rescued by a large group of Karankawa, who had never seen a European. The local people had no food with them at the first meeting but soon were visiting each day in the morning and evening with sustenance. The Karankawa eventually took the Spanish back to their village, carrying them by their armpits such that their feet did not touch the ground. As Cabeza de Vaca describes:

> Against the cold, and lest on the way someone of us might faint or die, they had provided four or five big fires on the road, at each one of which they warmed us. As soon as they saw we had regained a little warmth and strength they would carry us to the next fire with such haste that our feet barely touched the ground. So we got to their dwellings, where we saw they had built a hut for us with many fires in it. About one hour after our arrival, they began to dance and to have a great celebration (which lasted the whole night), although there was neither pleasure, feast nor sleep in it for us, since we expected to be sacrificed. In the morning they again gave us fish and roots, and treated us so well that we became reassured, losing somewhat our apprehension of being butchered [Bandelier 1905, 60].

In time, the Spaniards were given the work of women, pulling up submerged roots from rushes. It was a terrible, backbreaking job in the bitter cold. The reeds sliced into their hands, and they were mostly naked. As Cartwright (1998, 33) describes the condition of Cabeza de Vaca:

> Hunger and abject misery were his only companions, and his only choice was to submit himself in total obedience to the savages. Ten months earlier he had landed on the coast of Florida under the banner of the sovereign, the emperor Charles V, vowing to subject such savages to the cross and sword; now he himself was subjected to an even harsher imperialistic mandate, the law of nature. To his credit, Cabeza de Vaca accepted his fate with courage and humility.

De Vaca Makes a Startling Discovery

Early during the winter with the Karankawa, Cabeza de Vaca and the other survivors made a startling discovery. As he relates:

> I saw on one of the Indians a trinket he had not gotten from us, and asking from where they had obtained it they answered, by signs, that other men like ourselves and who were still in our rear, had given it to them. Hearing this, I sent two Christians with two Indians to guide them to those people. Very nearby they met them, and they also were looking for us, as the Indians had told them of our presence in the neighborhood. These were Captains Andres Dorantes and Alonso del Castillo, with all of their crew. When they came near us they were much frightened at our appearance and grieved at being unable to give us anything, since they had nothing but their clothes. And they stayed with us there, telling how, on the fifth of that same month, their barge stranded a league and a half from there, and they escaped without anything being lost [Bandelier 1905, 61–62].

Soon after the two groups of Spaniards were reunited, they repaired the barge, and the four most able-bodied were sent to seek out the settlement of Pánuco in New Spain, which they thought must be close by. As Cabeza de Vaca describes:

> One of them was a Portuguese, called Alvaro Fernández, a carpenter and sailor; the second was Mendez; the third, Figueroa, a native of Toledo; the fourth, Astudillo, from Zafra. They were all good swimmers and took with them an Indian from the island [Bandelier 1905, 63].

A few days after their compatriots left, never to be heard from again, the weather became so cold that they could no longer pull weeds or fish. A plague came next, probably cholera, that killed at least half of the Amerindians and Spaniards. Many others succumbed to starvation and exposure. Some of the Spanish resorted to cannibalism. As Cabeza de Vaca relates:

> A few days after these four Christians had left, the weather became so cold and tempestuous that the Indians could no longer pull roots, and the canebrake in which they used to fish yielded nothing more. As the lodges afforded so little shelter, people began to die, and five Christians, quartered on the coast, were driven to such an extremity that they ate each other up until but one remained, being left alone, there was nobody to eat him. Their names are: Sierra, Diego, Lopez, Corral, Palacios and Gonzalo Ruiz. At this the Indians were so startled, and there was such an uproar among them, that I verily believe if they had seen this at the beginning, they would have killed them, and we all would have been in great danger. After a very short time, out of eighty men who had come there in our two parties only fifteen remained alive [Bandelier 1905, 63].

Finally, the weather broke in late April, and everybody went on shore to gorge themselves on blackberries and oysters, dance incessantly, and celebrate.

Then came a long period of captivity when the Spaniards were inexplicably made shamans. Cabeza de Vaca left his captors in 1530 and lived alone for the next two years, wandering and trading with local groups. As Cartwright (1998, 36) describes it:

> Cabeza de Vaca became a bearded curiosity who stayed among them at various times of the year, bringing news and trade goods and a manner that was unfailingly ingratiating. Wherever he went, Cabeza de Vaca was welcome and well-treated. He was like one of them. He was as naked as they were, and he understood their customs and common phrases. He took part in their raids and moonlight rituals and learned to drink a bitter, mildly hallucinogenic tea that the Indians brewed from yaupon leaves and evergreen branches. He could have headed for Pánuco anytime he wished but Cabeza de Vaca couldn't bring himself to desert his addled and cowardly crewman, Lope de Oviedo. Each year he returned to the Island and each year Lope found a new excuse to stay put.

Finally, in the summer of 1532, Lope agreed to leave and accompany de Vaca in his annual wanderings down the coast. Along the route, they made the astonishing discovery near Port O'Connor, on the southern tip of Matagorda Bay, that three other members of the Narváez expedition were still alive and were prisoners of what de Vaca called the *Quevenes* nation. They have been identified with the Cujane Indians, a

Karankawan group (Campbell 1995). Andrés Dorantes, Alonso del Castillo, and the Moor slave Estebanico had been held for more than three years in cruel captivity. Cabeza de Vaca decided to join them, while Lope decided to head back to the Karankawas. Cabeza de Vaca was happy to let poor Lope go, having found other Spanish companions. Lope was never heard from again.

De Vaca Makes His Escape

For more than a year the three Spaniards and the Moor lived as slaves. Like their captors, they ate mostly roots, but also consumed anything organic including ant eggs, caterpillars, lizards, snakes, and spiders. They also became the first Europeans to eat buffalo. Cabeza de Vaca states:

> Cattle came here, and I have seen them three times, and partaken of them. It seems to me that they are the size of those of Spain. They have small horns ... and very long hair, flocky, like a merino's. Some are tawny, others black, and it seems to me that they have better and fatter meat than those of [Spain]. From the smaller ones the Indians make blankets to cover themselves, and from the larger ones they make shoes and shields. They come from the North over the land to the coast, spreading out over all the country more than four hundred leagues, and along their route and the valleys by which they come, the people who live nearby descend upon them and live off them [Bandelier 1905, 94].

The last four members of the expedition marked time and waited for a chance to flee. The opportunity arose in the spring of 1535, during a summer gathering of the various nations to feast on prickly pear cactus fruit. Cabeza de Vaca and the other Spaniards slipped away into the desert and headed south toward the Rio Grande.

Unfortunately for them, near the present Mexican border town of Reynosa instead of turning southeast to the Gulf where they would have found Spanish settlements in a few weeks, they headed west into the rugged Sierra Madre mountains, and then northeast, crossing the Rio Grande. They drifted through the rugged Big Bend region. From there they went north along the Chihuahuan Desert and crossed the Rio Grande again near El Paso del Norte.

The four survivors' trip had been a circuitous route that covered nearly 2,400 miles over eight years. Finally, in December 1535, as they trudged along the edge of the Sierra Madre mountains near Culiacán in present-day Sinaloa, they came upon the work of Spanish slave hunters. They found entire villages that were pillaged and burned and groups of captives who were chained together and herded by mounted conquistadors. De Vaca and his ragged companions were back on the frontier of "Christian civilization" (Cartwright 1998).

The Spaniards took the four survivors to Mexico City. Estevanico would become a guide for other expeditions, while de Vaca returned to Spain and wrote the full account of his journey. It would become the primary source of information about the Indigenous people of Texas.

The expedition of Narváez had turned out to be a complete nightmare. Out of the 300 men who accompanied him, only four survived. The animosity caused by Narváez's ruthless treatment of the Indigenous people and that of Ponce de León was so great that it delayed the Spanish settlement in Florida for years.

Lifeways of the Safety Harbor People, Apalachee, and Karankawa

Safety Harbor People

Soon after landing in Florida, the Narváez expedition encountered the Safety Harbor people, who lived on the central Gulf Coast of the Florida peninsula (Hann 2003; Milanich 1989 and 1995). This culture is noted for its burial mounds decorated with ceramics covered with a distinctive set of designs and symbols.

When Narváez reached Tampa Bay, there were three or four chiefdoms on the shores of the bay: Tocobaga at the northwest arm of Tampa Bay, Uzita at the south shore of Tampa Bay, and the Mocoso on the east side of Tampa Bay. The Mocoso people may have spoken Timucua. There may also have been a fourth chiefdom, Capaloey or Pohoy, on the northeast arm of the bay.

When the Narváez expedition first hit ground, they clashed with the Uzita before they headed inland through Tocobaga territory. The de Soto expedition would also land in Uzita territory in 1539 and then pass through Mocoso territory. Pedro Menéndez would visit the region in 1567; however, by this time, the Uzita and Mocoso chiefdoms had disappeared, and the Tocobaga dominated.

The culture is named after the site at Safety Harbor, Florida, which has the largest mound in the Tampa Bay region. The Safety Harbor people were organized into chiefdoms that were broken into four social classes including chiefs, headmen, warriors, and ordinary people and slaves. They lived primarily in villages along the shoreline. Each town contained a temple mound and a central plaza.

Atop the temple mounds was a wooden, thatched structure called a charnel house adorned with wooden bird carvings, where defleshed bones of the dead were kept until burial. At periodic intervals, the bones were wrapped in painted deer hide and buried in the subfloor of the charnel house. The charnel house was then removed, a new layer of soil was placed over the old, and a new charnel house was built.

The Safety Harbor people were primarily hunter-gatherers who ate a wide variety of foods including fish, shellfish, deer, turtles, manatee, dogs, watercress, pumpkins, cabbage palms, and some beans and maize. Their primary source of calories was fish and shellfish. They may have grown a little corn, but the southern limit of extensive maize cultivation was just north of Tampa Bay.

To hunt they used bows and arrows tipped with stone arrowheads or stingray stingers. They used conch shells tied to a wooden handle to make an axe. To dig clams, they constructed a special tool by sticking a living tree branch through a shell with a hole in it, and after the branch grew into the shell, it was cut off. They hunted with a throwing stick called an *atlatl* and disguised themselves by wearing deerskins or sometimes deer heads to get close enough to their prey to kill them.

Apalachee

After interacting with the Safety Harbor People, the Narváez expedition had considerable contact with the Apalachee. The Apalachee lived in an area extending between the Aucilla and Ochlockonee Rivers and from the Georgia state line to the Gulf of Mexico (McEwan 2004; Ricky 2001). At the time of the first European contact, there were 50,000 to 60,000 Apalachee.

The Apalachee were mound builders. Their largest settlement, at Lake Jackson north of Tallahassee, consisted of seven massive earthen mounds, some of which had structures on top. The largest mound within each village complex was the site of the chief's house.

The Apalachee were agriculturalists who lived in dispersed villages and grew corn, beans, squash, amaranth, and sunflower. The men prepared the fields for planting, and the women tended the crops. The men also hunted bear, deer, small game, wild turkeys, and mountain lions. The women gathered nuts and berries as well as cabbage palm and saw palmetto. For clothing, the men wore deerskin loincloths, and the women wore skirts of Spanish moss. The men painted their bodies with red ochre for battle and put feathers in their hair.

They had a complex, highly stratified society of regional chiefdoms. Each village had a war chief and a peace chief; leadership was hereditary and matrilineal. The Apalachee tools were made from stone, bone, and shell. They produced pottery, woven cloth, and cured deerskin. They used palm leaves or the bark of cypress or poplar trees to build their houses. They stored dried maize and beans in pits lined with mats, and they smoked meat on racks over fires. Hernando de Soto found enough stored food to feed his 600 men for five months when he took over the village of Anhaica in 1539.

The Apalachee played a game with a ball that was as much a religious exercise as a sport. One village would challenge another to a match, with up to 50 players on each team. Players would propel a clay, buckskin-covered ball about the size of a golf ball with their feet toward the goal, a stuffed eagle in a nest on top of a pole. The game was played in the spring and summer and was dedicated to the gods of rain and thunder, to ensure irrigation for their crops.

Karankawa

Da Vaca spent the bulk of his time in Mexico among the Karankawa. The Karankawa lived in southern Texas along the Gulf of Mexico, concentrated in the lower Colorado River and Brazos River Valleys (Lipscomb and Seiter 1976; Newcomb 2010). The name Karankawa is generally believed to mean "dog-lovers" or "dog-raisers."

The Karankawa were nomadic hunter-gatherers who traveled in groups of 30 to 40 people. They traveled from place to place in dugout canoes and generally camped close to the shoreline of a body of water. The canoes were quite roomy and could carry a whole family. Men stood on the stern and poled the canoes while the women, children, and their possessions traveled in the hold. The Karankawa also traveled overland by foot.

Their homes were a portable wigwam, or *ba-ak*, consisting of a willow pole frame that was covered with animal skins and rush mats. It was large enough to accommodate seven or eight people. The Karankawa crafted fine baskets and pottery, often lined with asphaltum, a tar-like substance from Gulf Coast beaches. The Karankawa ate venison, rabbit, fowl, fish, oysters and other shellfish, and turtles. They collected wild berries, persimmons, grapes, sea-bird eggs, nuts, and prickly pear cactus fruit and paddles.

The Karankawa were great archers, renowned for their skill on both land and in turbulent water. Their bows were made of red cedar wood and were built to match the height of each archer, reaching from the ground to the chin. They were also legendary runners and were known for their ability to communicate over long distances using smoke. These smoke signals were used to alert scattered groups to come together for social events and warfare.

Karankawa social life centered around gatherings which the Spaniards called *mitotes*.

> The ceremonies often included dances and the consumption of intoxicating beverages brewed from the parched leaves and berries of the yaupon (*Ilex cassine* or *vomitoria*), a small shrublike tree native to south Texas. One observer in the sixteenth century witnessed that the "black drink" was consumed exclusively by the men of the tribe. The Karankawas also participated in competitive games demonstrating weapons skills or physical prowess. Wrestling was so popular among Karankawas that neighboring tribes referred to them as the Wrestlers [Lipscomb and Seiter 1976].

The Karankawa groups were very loose-knit with separate leaders, only united by their common language and occasional joint war expeditions. The groups were led by two chiefs—a hereditary one who took care of civil affairs and a war leader, probably appointed by the civil government chief. The Karankawa were patrilocal, in which a married couple resides with the husband's parents (Ortiz 1978). They had an in-law taboo. Once a man and woman became married, the man and his children could no longer enter the home of his wife's parents, and the woman's parents could not enter his home. These two groups were not supposed to talk with one another, and if they came face to face, each party was to avert their eyes and move away.

Five

The Bloody Campaign of Hernando de Soto
1539–1543

Setting the Stage: One More Spanish Expedition in Search of Riches

While Cabeza de Vaca had seen little mineral wealth during his journey, he vaguely alluded to rumors of wealth that were north of his wanderings. The Spanish were not ready to give up the dream of finding additional wealth in North America.

Hernando de Soto would lead one of the most extraordinary expeditions to North America in 1539. He and his group journeyed for over four years in southeastern North America, savaging the local people and ultimately returning home empty-handed. They found the region to be filled with dozens of great agricultural societies, but there were no rich, glittering states to vanquish.

There are four written accounts of this expedition that provide a broad narrative of the expedition, including firsthand accounts by Rodrigo Ranjel, de Soto's private secretary, an unidentified Portuguese man named "the Gentleman of Elvas," and Luys Hernández de Biedma, who may have been a royal scribe (Clayton et al. 1995). Of these, Ranjel's account is generally considered the most reliable. There is also a secondhand account written by Garcilaso de la Vega, which is considered exaggerated. Scholars have added archaeological information over the last few decades to better "pinpoint" the route ("De Soto Trail: National historic trail study final report" 1990). Herein, I rely mostly on the account of Rodrigo Ranjel as it was recorded by Gonzalo Fernández de Oviedo y Valdés in his *Historia general y natural de las*

Indias (1526). I used a translation edited by Edward Gaylord Bourne in 1904.

Who Was Hernando Mendez de Soto?

Born in Jerez de los Caballeros in Extremadura, Spain, Hernando Mendez de Soto was the second son of wealthy parents. Since his older brother would inherit the family estate, he had to establish his own career. At the age of 14, de Soto went to Central America as a page for the first governor of Panama, Pedrarias "the Cruel" Dávila. As Dávila's representative, he explored Costa Rica and Honduras in search of treasure and land. He conquered Nicaragua in 1524 and was made the *alcalde*—or mayor—of León. In 1530, de Soto signed onto Pizarro's expedition to Peru. He would play an important role in the conquering of the Inca and would receive the third largest portion of the stolen wealth after Francisco Pizarro and his brother Hernando. De Soto was the first Spaniard to enter the capital of the Inca Empire, Cusco.

Now a very rich man, de Soto returned home in 1536 and married Isabel de Bobadilla, daughter of Dávila. Even though he was newly married and had a lovely home in Spain, he was restless and wanted to be a governor like Pizarro. In 1537 King Carlos I (Charles V of the Holy Roman Empire) granted de Soto an asiento to invade and settle La Florida. De Soto was given four years to conquer the "Indios" and to select 200 leagues of coast for his personal domain.

De Soto Heads to Florida

On April 7, 1538, de Soto and 650 men set sail from Seville, Spain, to La Habana, Cuba, and departed from there in May 1539 for Florida. The expedition included knights, foot soldiers, artisans, priests, boatwrights, and scribes, as well as 200 horses and a large herd of pigs. De Soto's primary mission was to find mineral wealth to enrich himself and his king.

He first landed on the west coast of Florida at the Amerindian chiefdom of Uzita of the Safety Harbor culture, probably in the Tampa Bay area. During the next few months, the expedition explored the area around their landing, then traveled north and northwest to Anhaica,

FIVE—The Bloody Campaign of Hernando de Soto

the principal town of the Apalachee chiefdom near present-day Tallahassee. Both these Indigenous people had been previously confronted by Pánfilo de Narváez in his disastrous expedition (Chapter 4).

Portrait of Hernando de Soto (circa 1500–1542); Engraving from Retratos de los Españoles Illustres con un Epítome de sus Vidas, Madrid, Imprenta real, 1791; Florida's Centennial, March 3, 1945 (Library of Congress / Wikimedia Commons).

From Ponce de León to Sir Walter Raleigh

Ranjel recounts:

> From the town of Ucita the Governor sent the Chief Castellan, Baltasar de Gallegos, into the country, with forty horsemen and eighty footmen, to procure an Indian if possible ... [these Indians] are exceedingly ready with their weapons ... warlike and nimble ... they never remain quiet, but are continually running, traversing from place to place ... before a Christian can make a single shot with either [crossbow or arquebus] an Indian will discharge three or four arrows; and he seldom misses of his object [Bourne 1904, 25–26].

This early exploration would set the pattern for the whole de Soto mission. At that time, the southeastern United States was densely packed with many different chiefdoms of farmers. De Soto would travel from one Indigenous community to another following local trails and camping near villages where stores of maize could be found. There he would demand or steal food and ask the local leaders where he could find gold, silver, or any other precious objects. The local leaders would almost always tell him that such riches were further down the road to get him out of their hair.

While other Spaniards often traded with the Amerindians, de Soto simply stole what he wanted. He carried no food supplies other than his herd of pigs (which he rarely slaughtered), and his army fed itself on maize taken from villagers, often putting them at risk of starvation. He also seized dozens of local men, women, and children to carry equipment and supplies, perform camp chores, and satisfy any other needs the army might have. Any resistance brought swift and cruel punishment. As told by Ranjel:

> This Governor was much given to the sport of slaying Indians, from the time that he went on military expeditions with the Governor Pedro Arias Dávila in the provinces of Castilla del Oro and of Nicaragua; and likewise when he was in Peru and present at the capture of that great Prince Atabalipa, where he was enriched [Bourne 1904, 59].

On one of their early forays from Uzita to explore the countryside, de Soto's army encountered a Spaniard, Juan Ortiz, who had been part of the Narváez expedition and had been held captive by the Apalachee for about 10 years. As told by Ranjel:

> The Governor sent Captain Baltasar de Gallegos with an Indian to look for some people or a village or a house. Toward sunset, being off their road, because the Indian, who was the guide, led them wandering and confused, it pleased God that they descried at a distance some twenty Indians painted

with a kind of red ointment that the Indians put on when they go to war or wish to make a fine appearance. They wore many feathers and had their bows and arrows. And when the Christians ran at them the Indians fled to a hill, and one of them came forth into the path lifting up his voice and saying—Sirs, for the love of God and of Holy Mary, slay not me; I am a Christian like yourselves and was born in Seville, and my name is Johan Ortiz [Bourne 1904, 56–57].

Ortiz provided de Soto with intelligence about the area around Tampa Bay and would continue to serve in a critical role as a translator.

Into Georgia

De Soto and his army spent the winter of 1539–40 in Anhaica and several nearby settlements. Here they took a hundred captives, put them in chains with collars around their necks, and required them to carry baggage and grind maize to feed the army. In the spring, the explorers headed north into Georgia with their slaves and meandered through South Carolina, North Carolina, and Tennessee before heading southwest through the northwestern corner of Georgia into central Alabama.

As de Soto's army entered what is now southern Georgia, it was forced to cross a large river, the Flint, which had been swollen by spring rains to dangerous levels. To cross, the army built a barge that they moved using a chain strung between the two shores. The chain broke twice, and the barge flew out of control, but, somehow, everyone made it across, and the expedition was able to continue north.

Near the end of March, around present-day Macon, Georgia, one of their native guides, named Perico, informed de Soto of a province named "Yupaha" that was ruled by a woman and rich in gold. He indicated that it was only a few days away. He was contradicted by several other captives, who warned de Soto that the area east of them was desolate and unpopulated and that he would risk starvation. Undaunted, dazzled by the promise of gold, de Soto chose to follow Perico's directions. He impressed 700 local people as servants and struck off eastward into the uninhabited wilderness. The trip would be one of unmitigated hardships.

On the fifth day of travel, they reached the Savannah River, which was swollen from spring rains, making the crossing treacherous. The mounted soldiers had a wild ride across the raging waters, holding their bridles tight, with the water lapping at their heels and saddlebags. The soldiers on foot linked arms together in a chain 30 to 40 feet long and slowly plodded together across the swirling waters.

The Lady of Cofitachequi

Landing exhausted but alive on the other side of the river, de Soto's soldiers faced another major crisis—they were almost out of food. All de Soto could do was order everyone to move faster on severely reduced rations, in hopes of finding food sooner. He increased their pace from 17 to 30 miles a day. As they staggered forward, they continued to be confronted by many more flooded rivers that required barges to cross.

On April 25, after two weeks of exhausting travel, the starving army finally came upon Cofitachequi, near Camden, South Carolina, a chiefdom that controlled most of the eastern half of South Carolina and North Carolina. This chiefdom ruled the coast where Francisco Chicora had been captured and Lucas Vázquez de Ayllón had tried to build his colony. De Soto likely knew of the legend of Chicora (Hoffman 1984). In Cofitachequi, de Soto found European axes and glass rosary beads, which the Spaniards believed had been obtained from members of the Ayllón expedition (Hudson et al. 1989).

De Soto was met by a woman the Spanish called the Lady of Cofitachequi (Waddell 2005). She invited the strangers to her village, where she presented de Soto with gifts of animal pelts, blankets, pearls, salt, venison, and other food, in a cordial welcoming ceremony. De Soto demanded gold and silver but was shown only copper and mica. Furious, he and his soldiers stormed to the top of a sacred mound and ransacked the temple. They found ornate chests containing the bones of honored ancestors as well as animal skins, furs, and pearls. The Spanish stole everything valuable they could carry, then kidnapped the Lady of Cofitachequi and headed north. They climbed through the mountains of North Carolina, where the Lady of Cofitachequi managed to escape.

The ever-weakening soldiers plodded on for many days, sometimes finding food but more often than not going hungry. Ranjel reported:

> In seven days the Governor arrived at the Province of Chelaque, the country poorest off for maize of any that was seen in Florida, where the inhabitants subsisted on the roots of plants that they dig in the wilds, and on the animals they destroy with their arrows.... From Ocute to Cutifachiqui are

one hundred and thirty leagues, of which eighty are desert; from Cuitifa to Xualla are two hundred and fifty miles of mountainous country; thence to Guaxule ... at the end of five days the Governor arrived at Guaxule.... The Christians being seen to go after dogs, for their flesh, which the Indians do not eat, they gave them three hundred of those animals. Little maize was found there, or anywhere upon that route....

He left Guaxule and after two days' travel arrived at Canasagua, where twenty men came out from the town on the road, each laden with a basket of mulberries. This fruit is abundant and good ... as are the walnut and the amiexa; the trees growing about over the country, without planting or pruning, of the size and luxuriance they would have were they cultivated in orchards, by hoeing and irrigation. Leaving Canasagua, he marched five days through a desert.... On the fifth day of July, the Governor entered Chiaha.... There was abundance of lard in calabashes, drawn like olive oil, which the inhabitants said was the fat of bear. There was likewise found much oil of walnuts, which, like the lard, was clear and of good taste; and also a honey-comb, which the Christians had never seen before [in Florida], nor saw afterward, nor honey, nor bees, in all the country [Bourne 1904, 69–74].

De Soto's expedition continued west, exploring parts of north Georgia and eastern Tennessee, but by now they were faced with almost continuous harassment from the Amerindians. They attacked the soldiers' camps swiftly in the night and then disappeared into the landscape. De Soto and his soldiers "grew increasingly despondent, as his futile search for gold dragged on, and his resources dwindled" ("Hernando de Soto" 2023).

A Bloody Battle at Mabila

As they entered central Alabama, they encountered the palisaded town of Mabila, where they were attacked by warriors of Chief Tuscaloosa. It was here that de Soto fought the greatest battle of his campaign (Hudson et al. 1989).

A fierce, day-long battle ensued in which 22 Spaniards were killed and 148 wounded, although Tuscaloosa took the brunt of the battle, losing 2,500 to 3,000 men.

As described by Ranjel:

There was great valor and shame that day among all those who found themselves in this first attack and beginning of this unhappy day; for they fought to admiration and each Christian did his duty as a most valiant soldier [Bourne 1904, 125].

The expedition remained in Mabila for about a month, the soldiers licking their wounds. De Soto and his army then traveled on to the lands of the Chickasaw, where they were encamped for the winter of 1540–41. En route, they contacted several Indigenous groups, including the Ichisi, Ocute, Coosa, and Tuscaloosa.

They were very well received at the chiefdom of Coosa covering eastern Tennessee, northwestern Georgia, and northern Alabama. It "seemed to De Soto's men to be one of the finest provinces in all of La Florida" (Hudson et al. 1989, 32).

The Coosa chose placation over warfare.

Attack by the Chickasaw

De Soto and his army spent a difficult winter at Chickasaw. The winter of 1540–1 was bitterly cold, they did not have adequate shelter, and their clothing was now threadbare and in short supply. The Chickasaw also kept them constantly on edge by waging guerrilla warfare against them, day and night.

Relations turned particularly sour when de Soto began plans to leave in the spring and demanded 200 burden-bearers to serve them on their travels. Just before dawn on March 4, the day the expedition planned to depart, several hundred Chickasaw attacked the Spanish and set fire to their camp. Twelve Spaniards, 59 horses, and hundreds of pigs died in the attack.

As Ranjel described the heat of the battle:

> And all the Spaniards fought like men of great courage, and twenty-two died, and one hundred and forty-eight others received six hundred and eighty-eight arrow wounds, and seven horses were killed, and twenty-nine others wounded. Women and even boys of four years of age fought with the Christians, Indian boys hanged themselves not to fall into their hands, and others jumped into the fire of their own accord. See with what good will those carriers acted. The arrow shots were tremendous and sent with such a will and force that the lance of one gentleman named Nuno de Tovar, made of two pieces of ash and very good, was pierced by an arrow in the middle, as by an auger, without being split, and the arrow made a cross with the lance.
>
> On that day there died Don Carlos, and Francis de Soto, the nephew of the Governor, and Johan de Gamez de Jaen, and Men Rodriguez, a fine Portuguese gentleman, and Espinosa, a fine gentleman, and another named Yelez, and one Blasco de Barcarrota, and many other honored soldiers; and

the wounded comprised all the men of most worth and honor in the army. They killed three thousand of the vagabonds without counting many others who were wounded and whom they afterward found dead in the cabins and along the roads. Whether the chief was dead or alive was never known. The son they found thrust through with a sword [Bourne 1904, 127–28].

The Mighty Mississippi and Its Environs

After taking some time to recover, the expedition moved out in a northwesterly direction through the chiefdoms of Alibamu and Quizquiz, along the way discovering the Mississippi River. Here they built rafts to cross the mighty river and, while crossing, were greeted by people from the chiefdom of Aquixo. These Amerindians arrived in a fleet of 200 canoes, each carrying 100 warriors who were decorated with colorful paints and feathers. Their leader presented de Soto with a gift of fish and plum loaves and claimed to represent the chief of Pacaha, whose province lay farther up the river. De Soto rebuffed this attempt at friendship by ordering his crossbowmen to fire upon the visitors, forcing them to withdraw, but not without gestures of great disdain.

When de Soto's group crossed over the Mississippi, the Spaniards came upon some of the most agriculturally productive land they were to see. Extensive fields of corn and groves of nut and fruit trees were observed located between fortified towns with populations in the thousands. Complex systems of roads and trails connected one town to the next. Many of the towns were filled with hundreds of square, thatch-covered houses and open plazas for public ceremonies. Large flat-topped earthen mounds supported leaders' residences and temples containing finely crafted artifacts and the remains of esteemed relatives.

Ranjel enthusiastically reported:

> This land is higher, drier, and more level than any other along the river ... in the fields were many walnut trees, bearing tender-shelled nuts in the shape of acorns, many being found stored in the houses. The tree did not differ in anything from that of Spain, nor from the one seen before, except the leaf was smaller. There were many mulberry trees and trees of ameixas, having fruit of vermillion hue, like one of Spain, while others were gray, differing, but far better ... the Chief sent [the soldiers] a present of skins, shawls, and fish ... and the inhabitants awaited him in peace, offering him skins, shawls, and fish [Bourne 1904, 116–18].

On Wednesday, the nineteenth day of June, the Governor entered Pacaha.... From the [Mississippi] to the lake was a canal, through which the fish came into it, and where the Chief kept them for his eating and pastime.... In the many other lakes about were also many fish, though the flesh was soft, and none of it so good as that which came from the river. The greater number differs from those in the freshwater of Spain. There was a fish called bagre [i.e., catfish] the third part of which was head, with gills from end to end, and along the sides were great spines, like very sharp awls ... in the river were some that weighed from one hundred to one hundred and fifty pounds. Many were taken with the hook. There was one in the shape of a barbel; another like bream, with the head of a hake, having a color between red and brown, and was the most esteemed. There was likewise a kind called peel-fish, the snout a cubit in length, the upper lip being shaped like a shovel. Another fish was like a shad.... There was one, called pereo, which the Indians sometimes brought, the size of a hog, and had rows of teeth above and below [Bourne 1904, 123–24].

Central Arkansas and the Great Plains

De Soto and the expedition headed through central Arkansas and met the chiefdoms of Casqui, Pacaha, Quiguate, Coligua, Cayas, and Tula. When they reached the Arkansas River Valley, de Soto and company found unfortified, dispersed villages composed of individual farmsteads, but these villages were also organized "around ceremonial centers featuring the plazas, mounds, and temples that characterize sixteenth-century communities across the Southeast" (Sabo 2023).

In this region, they were entering into the territorial fringes of the Great Plains, where the local people were buffalo hunters. The Casqui were very welcoming and gave the Spaniards food and buffalo hides as gifts, even though they had been suffering themselves under a prolonged drought. Ranjel observed that "this was the most populous of any country that was seen in Florida, and the most abundant in maize, excepting Coça and Apalachee" (Bourne 1904, 146–49). The chief of Casqui also offered de Soto his daughter to wed, saying that his greatest desire was to unite his blood with that of so great a leader as he.

The Casqui were then instructed by the expedition's priests about their Christian God. Upon hearing this sermon, the chief pleaded with the priests to pray for rain. De Soto had a large cross erected on their temple mound, and the priests conducted a religious ceremony. Incredibly, it rained the following day.

The emboldened Casqui then asked the Spaniards to join them in an attack on the rival Pacaha chiefdom, claiming they possessed gold. A combined force of Spanish soldiers and Casqui warriors routed Pacaha's main town, but the Spanish again found no gold.

De Soto and his army continued their travels and arrived in early November at Autiamque, located on the south side of the Arkansas River between today's Little Rock and Pine Bluff. Here they spent another bitter cold winter, during which they were completely snowbound for a month. By then 250 of his men and 150 horses had died. Their interpreter Juan Ortiz also died that winter, and from this point on their communication with the Indigenous peoples became extremely difficult.

The expedition set out from Autiamque in early March 1542 and traveled to the chiefdom of Anilco, located along the Arkansas River, just above its confluence with the Mississippi. Anilco was one of the most densely populated chiefdoms encountered by de Soto on his trip. Growing increasingly frustrated at the condition of his army and its failure to find gold, de Soto sent a message to the local chief, demanding that he appear and offer tribute. When the chief refused, de Soto flew into a rage and ordered a brutal attack, slaughtering hundreds of men, women, and children.

De Soto Sickens and Dies

Just before the attack, de Soto fell ill with a fever and was unable to lead it. He died a few days later at the age of 42, and Luis de Moscoso Alvarado succeeded him as captain general. Ranjel relates:

> The Governor sank into a deep despondency at the sight of the difficulties that presented themselves to his reaching the sea.... The Governor was already low, being very ill of fevers ... the twenty-first of May [1542], departed this life the magnanimous, the virtuous, the intrepid Captain, Don Hernando de Soto, Governor of Cuba and Adelantado of Florida ... he died in a land, and at a time, that could afford him little comfort in his illness.... So soon as the death had taken place, Luys de Moscoso [de Alvarado] directed the body to be put secretly into a house, where it remained three days; and thence it was taken at night, by his order, to a gate of the town, and buried within. The Indians, who had seen him ill, finding him no longer, suspected the reason; and passing by where he lay, they observed the ground loose, and, looking about, talked among themselves.

This coming to the knowledge of Luys de Moscoso, he ordered the corpse to be taken up at night, and among the shawls that enshrouded it having cast an abundance of sand, it was taken out in a canoe and committed to the middle of the stream.... Luys de Moscoso ordered the property of the Governor to be sold at public outcry. It consisted of two male and three female slaves, three horses, and seven hundred swine.... From that time forward most of the people owned and raised hogs; they lived on pork, observed Fridays and Saturdays, and the vespers of holidays, which they had not done before; for, at times, they had passed two or three months without tasting any meat, and on the day they got any, it had been their custom to eat it [Bourne 1904, 154–64].

The Survivors Head Home

After de Soto's death, the remaining members of the expedition debated on how to get to New Spain (Mexico) and end the mission. They could escape by either land or river. They first chose the land route but soon abandoned this approach as they had difficulty finding enough corn to sustain themselves along the trail. They went back to the Mississippi and chose as their jumping-off point Aminoya, where there were two palisaded towns. One of these they moved into and the other they tore down to build their ships.

On the morning of July 2, they started down the river. In addition to the current, each boat was propelled by seven pairs of oars and a sail that unfurled when the wind was right. Their progress was rapid, and on the first day they went 48 miles before mooring for the night near the mouth of the Arkansas River.

The next day, they came to Huhasene, under the domain of the chieftain Quigualtam, and expropriated a large supply of maize from the granaries of his village. This infuriated the chief, and the following morning he attacked the Spanish with a fleet of 100 large war canoes. The warriors continued the attack all that day and throughout the night, with the Spaniards fleeing down the river as fast as they could. Finally, around noon on July 5, Quigualtam ordered the canoes to head back home, as they had apparently reached the end of their territory. No sooner had this attack ended than another chief sent a second fleet of 50 large canoes to confront the Spaniards. This chase lasted another day and night until these combatants disengaged.

Now near the present-day city of Natchez, the Spanish were finally left alone, probably because they were no longer passing along the territory of any more powerful chiefdoms. Moscoso and his men reached the mouth of the Mississippi River 12 days later, having traveled between 400 and 500 river miles. From there they sailed and rowed along the Gulf Coast and, 53 days later on September 10, 1543, arrived at the mouth of the Pánuco River in Mexico, where there was a Spanish settlement. Here the de Soto expedition ended after four years and four months, with about half the army surviving. The explorers had walked, ridden, and sailed for well over five thousand miles.

Legacy of the de Soto Expedition

At the time, the de Soto expedition was considered a failure, since they did not find a state-level society with stores of precious metals and gems like those possessed by the Incas and Aztecs. The Spanish interest in the region waned, and it would be left to France and England in the mid–seventeenth century to pursue imperial designs in the interior Southeast. However, the de Soto expedition was successful in many other ways. Subsequent expeditions into the southeastern interior during the latter half of the sixteenth century and beyond relied heavily on the knowledge generated by this expedition.

> It was the De Soto expedition that first succeeded in penetrating and exploring the vast interior areas of the southeastern United States. As the first Europeans to see the interior of the continent, the De Soto expedition is comparable in significance to the Coronado Expedition (1540–42) which explored the western United States. Written accounts of the journey contain the only descriptions of the people who inhabited the region prior to European contact. Further, expedition reports about the land later helped stimulate colonization ["De Soto Trail: National historic trail study final report" 1990, 14].

The de Soto expedition is also historically important because the participants observed and left records of many Indigenous societies while they were still intact. These societies were beginning to struggle, troubled by internal instability and external competition, and were starting to fracture and recombine. Their population numbers were also greatly decimated by the diseases brought onto them by the long, extensive de Soto expedition.

One More Tragedy in the Wake of de Soto

A Dominican priest, Luis de Cáncer, met a tragic end trying to undo the damage caused by de Soto's ruthless onslaught on the Indigenous people (Burnett 1986). After serving successfully as a missionary in Puerto Rico and Hispaniola, he was sure that nonviolence was the key to success in converting the Indigenous people. He proposed to King Charles V that he undertake a peaceful mission to Florida, which was accepted with the proviso that he would avoid the hostile territory in the upper east coast that had been riled up by de Soto and previously Ponce and Narváez.

Cáncer recruited four Dominicans: Gregorio de Beteta, Diego de Tolosa, Juan García, and Brother Fuentes. Leaving Veracruz, they reached Havana in 1549. There they picked up a converted Amerindian named Magdalena as an interpreter. The group then headed for Florida, but instead of avoiding the Gulf Coast, they landed right in the middle of an area south of Tampa Bay where Narváez had begun his expedition. Remarkably, Cáncer's group was first greeted peacefully by a receptive group of Amerindians, who suggested they should begin their work in a nearby Tocobaga village. Magdalena, with de Tolosa, Fuentes, and an unknown soldier, set off on foot, while Cáncer returned to the ship planning to meet the group further down the bay.

When the ship reached the shore near the village site, only Magdalena and a group of Tocobaga greeted them. Magdalena, now in Indigenous attire, claimed that she had convinced the local cacique that the monks came in peace and that they were now his guests. But soon after, another Spaniard appeared at the ship who had been a captive of the Tocobaga. The man delivered the tragic news that the two missionaries had been killed and the sailor enslaved.

Beteta and García wanted to flee to a safer harbor, but Cáncer was resolved to continue his mission. The next day the three rowed to a place, where they saw a group of Tocobaga. Cáncer waded to shore, got on his knees to pray, and then was clubbed to death. Peaceful interaction was no longer possible between the Spanish and the Indigenous people of Tampa Bay.

Five—The Bloody Campaign of Hernando de Soto

Lifeways of the Indigenous People Met by de Soto

In his long, bloody trek de Soto interacted with groups of the Safety Harbor People, Apalachee, Calusa, and Timucua that Ponce de León and Narváez had previously encountered, and he came across dozens more societies scattered across the huge area he covered in southeastern and central North America. De Soto and his soldiers had their most extensive interactions with the Apalachee and Uzita in Florida, Cofitachequi in South Carolina, Coosa in Georgia, Anilco, Aquixo, Casqui, Chickasaw, Huhasene, and Pacaha in Arkansas, and Tuscaloosa in Alabama (Hudson 1976 and 1997).

Most of the groups encountered by de Soto were bands and chiefdoms belonging to the very widespread Mississippian culture, all very similar to the Apalachee of the Florida panhandle, already described in Chapter 4. These groups shared several cultural characteristics, including: (1) the construction of large, earthwork mounds that were usually square, rectangular, or more rarely circular, with houses and temples built on top; (2) the clearing of fields by burning areas of forest and growth of maize, beans, squash, and sunflowers in plots worked by hand with shell or stone hoes; (3) the construction of shell-tempered pottery; (4) trade across a widespread network that extended from the Rocky Mountains to the Atlantic Ocean and from the Great Lakes to the Gulf of Mexico; (5) centralized control through a chiefdom with a high level of social complexity; and (6) a settlement hierarchy where one major center controlled a number of lesser communities (Blitz 2007; Hirst 2021).

Settlements were concentrated in river valleys, with their rich soils and abundant wild foods. The people lived in fortified towns or small homesteads. The Mississippian culture had no writing system and did not have stone architecture. They worked metal like copper into ritual objects and decorations but did not smelt iron or conduct bronze metallurgy. Their houses were small, one-room buildings, which slept two or three people. The walls were made of vertical logs, often set in foundation trenches, and covered with cane wattles, grass thatch, or sometimes a mud-and-straw plaster.

Two of the Indigenous people encountered by de Soto, the Cofitachequi and Coosa, would play extremely important roles in the later expeditions of Tristán de Luna y Arellano (Chapter 6) and Juan Pardo (Chapter 9). The early Spanish explorers considered the Coosa to be one of the most important chiefdoms in the Southeast (Hudson et al. 1985). It consisted of eight towns along the Coosawattee River in Georgia. Its capital, now known as Little Egypt, was a large city that consisted of three earthen mounds surrounding an open plaza area (Smith 2019). Its population was between 2,500 and 4,650 people. The chiefdom of Coosa was part of a much larger political organization that spanned from upper eastern Tennessee to east-central Alabama. It ruled as many as 50,000 people in seven other similar chiefdoms, spanning a distance of about 400 miles.

The Cofitachequi represented one of the highest material cultures encountered by the de Soto expedition. Their principal city of Talomeco was a large town of 500 houses, and their cacique, when de Soto visited, was obeyed across an area encompassing 260 miles (Waddell 2005). In Garcilaso de la Vega's chronicle of the de Soto expedition published in 1605, he wrote that the funerary temple at Talomeco, was "the richest and most superb of all those that our Spaniards saw in La Florida," measuring 250 paces long and 100 paces wide (Waddell 2005, 306). It was covered by woven mats instead of thatch like all the other buildings in the Southeast, making it distinctive from other Indigenous structures across Florida and Georgia. "On the roof of the temple there had been placed many shells ... with the inner side on top because of its greater luster ... large skins made of strings and pearls half a fathom long ... were spread out on the roof" (Waddell 2005, 334). Inside the temple were six pairs of carved wooden figures, the largest being 11 feet tall. "The corpses of former chiefs and their closest relatives were inside wooden sepulchers raised on benches that were placed against the walls" (Waddell 2005, 336). Great sacks of pearls were at their necks.

Six

The Luna Colony and the Coosa
1559–1561

Setting the Stage: The Route of the Treasure Fleets

In the sixteenth century, annual convoys were organized for the precious cargo headed to Spain from Veracruz (Mexico), Nombre de Dios (Panama), and Cartagena (Colombia). The armed convoys headed first to Havana, obtaining supplies and taking on more cargo. The typical ship traveling from Veracruz to Havana was forced to sail north to northeast along the Mexican coast to the northern limits of the Gulf of Mexico and then would steer along the northern coast and then go south past Tampa Bay on their way to Havana. The ships leaving Havana for Spain would then travel through the Straits of Florida and then ride the Gulf Stream across the Atlantic, turning east at the Sea Islands of Georgia and South Carolina.

The journey of the richly laden galleons along the peninsula of Florida was fraught with danger. The Florida Gulf Coast became the final resting place for many homebound Spanish ships caught by buffeting winds and hurricanes. They were also preyed upon by the corsairs of Spain's rivals from hideouts in the Bahamas.

Padre Island Shipwrecks of 1554

On April 9, 1554, four ships left San Juan de Ulúa with Antonio Corzo as captain-general. The ships were filled with precious cargo valued at well over 10 million dollars, including resins, sugar, wood, cowhides, and cochineal, as well as gold bars and silver bullion. Twenty days later, three of the four vessels (the *Santa María de Yciar, the Espíritu Santo,* and the *San Esteban*) were lost in a storm on Padre Island, 50 miles south of Corpus Christi Bay. Only one ship escaped, the *San Andrés.* It managed to limp to Havana but in such poor condition that it was scrapped, and its cargo was transferred to other vessels to be shipped to Spain.

About 300 people were on the shipwrecked vessels, and up to two-thirds of them drowned. The master of *San Esteban*, Francisco del Huerto, was able to salvage a boat and sailed for Veracruz with a few seamen to inform officials of the disaster. A second, larger group of survivors tried to hike along the beach back to New Spain, but it turned into a death march with only one survivor, Fray Marcos de Mena, reaching Pánuco (Weddle 1985).

The survivors were murdered one by one by the Karankawa as they marched along. In the beginning, they offered the survivors fish to eat but soon after attacked them at their campsite. Some Spaniards tried to placate the Amerindians by stripping off their clothes.

> Without even that meager protection, the group faced even greater hardships—mosquitoes and hot sands. Many traveled with wounds from Indian arrows, including Fray Marcos de Mena, who was shot seven times. His companions, thinking death was imminent, buried him in the sand, leaving only his head exposed. Revived by the warmth of the sand, he crawled from his "grave" and made his way along the coast. Friendly natives helped him make his way to Panuco [Drolet and Stryker, n.d.].

When word of the disaster reached Mexico City in early June, the viceroy sent conquistador Ángel de Villafañe marching overland to Pánuco to hire a ship and find the remains of the treasure-laden vessels. By the time he got there, Captain García de Escalante Alvarado had already left Veracruz for the site of the wrecks with six salvage vessels. The two teams labored together until September 12 to recover as much of the cargo as possible. All in all, the two were able to salvage about 40 percent of the cargo, 35,805 out of at least 51,000 pounds (Arnold and Wickman 2021). This tragedy, on top of many other shipwrecks across the Gulf of Mexico and Florida Strait, would spur interest in establishing colonies along the route of the treasure fleets to support shipping and more rapidly respond to shipwreck disasters.

Six—The Luna Colony and the Coosa

A Settlement Plan Is Hatched

When Philip II of Spain succeeded his father in 1556, It was clear to him that "a port of refuge, rescue, and salvage was needed on the mainland, and it should also be armed for protection from the French" (Sauer 1971, 191). An initial decision was made to make a settlement in the area representing Chicora, where Lucas Vázquez de Ayllón's colony had failed in 1526. In Francisco López de Gómara's *General History of the Indies* in 1552, he referred to the area as "a land" (*una tierra*) or "one land" called "Chicora and Gualdape which is at 32° North and is that which is now called the Cape of Santa Elena and River Jordan" (Hoffman 1983, 64).

A colony at Punta de Santa Helena could offer protection to Spanish ships as they passed through the Bahama Channel and would "make it impossible for France to validate her claim to the region after the voyage of Giovanni da Verrazzano" (Hudson 1988, 599). It would also allow the Spanish to continue searching the region for gold and precious gems, based on the rumors still left over from the de Soto mission and earlier reports from the slavers working around Chicora.

Luis de Velasco, who was now the viceroy of New Spain, was directed by Philip II to "equip, direct and pay for the new settlement" (Sauer 1971, 192). Tristán de Luna y Arellano was named governor of Florida and charged with setting up the colony. He was an experienced soldier, having served as a commander in the Coronado expedition into the southwestern United States.

Velasco proposed a broad plan:

> Santa Anna Elena was, he wrote, distant 170 leagues from Havana and 460 from Vera Cruz by a circuitous route. It would be better, to begin with a settlement in the northeast of the Gulf of Mexico, on a bay such as Narváez had used when he built the barges for his escape. From here, a land route could be laid across the peninsula to Santa Elena, passing through a populous country only about 80 leagues long.... A Gulf port, connected to Santa Elena by a road across the base of the Florida Peninsula, would shorten the distance, avoid the hazards of the exposed Atlantic coast, and occupy a land of Indian farmers suitable for colonization. Also, being on the Gulf of Mexico, it was beyond the range of corsairs [Sauer 1971, 192].

From this suggestion, a colonial plan evolved in which a town would be established by Luna at Ochuse in Pensacola Bay, where de Soto had previously landed (Chapter 5). From there, a route would be forged to Coosa in Alabama, the capital of a particularly powerful and friendly polity that had also been visited by de Soto. A road would then be built from Coosa to a harbor near Punta de Santa Elena in South Carolina. If these goals could be accomplished, all the dispersed areas of La Florida that had been visited by Spanish explorers would be linked, blocking any French claims to it.

> On paper, it seemed to be a good plan, but it became a nightmare when Luna tried to carry it out. The Spaniards were misinformed about both the land and the native people. The distances between Ochuse, Coosa, and the Punta de Santa Elena were much greater than the Spaniards realized, and the native people were fewer in number and less manageable. The Luna expedition was destined to fail [Hudson 1988, 600].

The Expedition

There are two excellent detailed, early accounts of the Luna expedition. A two-volume collation of all the principal documents translated by Herbert Ingram Priestley (1928), *The Luna Papers: Documents Relating to the Expedition of Don Tristán de Luna y Arellano for the Conquest of La Florida in 1559–1561*, and Fray Agustín Dávila Padilla's (1598) *Historia de la fundación y discurso de la provincia de Santiago de México de la orden de Predicadores*. The latter contains reports from Fray Domingo de la Anunciación, who was a member of the expedition. Translated portions of this account are contained in John R. Swanton's (1922) *Early History of the Creek Indians and Their Neighbors*, Bureau of American Ethnology Bulletin 73. There are also two excellent modern summaries of the expedition: C. Hudson's (1988) "A Spanish-Coosa Alliance in Sixteenth-Century North Georgia" and Hudson et al.'s (1989) "The Tristán de Luna Expedition, 1559–1561." Herein, I quote freely from Priestley's and Swanton's translations.

On June 11, 1559, Luna set sail from Veracruz with a fleet of 13 ships. On board were about 500 soldiers, one thousand colonists, and a large group of Aztec farmers and craftsmen. The expedition also started with 240 horses, although 100 died before they arrived.

They made their first landfall 31 days later at a place they called Bahía de Miruelo (today's Apalachee Bay). There they took water, wood, and food for the horses, and sent out a frigate to look for Ochuse. After some searching, it was found about 180 kilometers from Bahía de Miruelo, and the Luna party landed there and set about establishing their colony, which they named Polonza. It is not known why they chose this name.

> They unloaded household items and equipment: plain, white-glazed majolica dishes from Spain, earthenware olive jars that carried vinegar, wine, oil or water, armor, and nails. They brought ashore some provisions. They tended their horses. Two groups set off to explore the interior. Luna sent a ship back to Veracruz, their point of beginning, to inform the viceroy that the expedition had safely arrived [Holloway 2016].

Then, on September 19, a furious hurricane struck. Of Luna's remaining fleet of 12 ships, all except three were sunk or run ashore. About half of their supplies, including food, were lost, and an unknown number of colonists were killed.

> It blew from various directions for twenty-four hours, snapping the moorings of the ships, breaking them up, sinking them, or running them aground. Dávila Padilla tells how one of the ships was driven into a clump of brushwood an arquebuse shot's distance from shore and left there unhurt. The expeditionary went to see it as a prodigy, and each man brought away everything bearing his mark, for not a pin, was missing.... Dávila gravely asserts that the water could not have carried the ship so far inland, and it must have been the work of demons, for they were seen in the air during the storm. Demons of hunger all were now to see, Luna, first of all, struggling to forefend it by dispatching a party inland promptly and by deciding to move his expedition thither before habilitating the port, for it now became a dire necessity to live upon the resources of the inhospitable and unpromising country until the food supply lost in the hurricane could be replaced from Mexico or Spain [Priestley 1928, xxxvi].

The Colonists Disperse

The hurricane left the Luna party in dire straits, as there were few Indigenous people living around Pensacola Bay from whom to obtain food by trade or force. Luna realized that he would have to move his colonists to more populated regions in the interior where food could be procured. He simply had too many mouths to feed.

From the de Soto expedition, Luna would have known of two Amerindian villages on the Alabama River, Mabila and Piachi, about 40 leagues to the north of where they had landed. Mabila had been destroyed by de Soto after his battle with Tuscaloosa, but he had passed by Piachi leaving it undamaged. In mid–September 1559, Luna sent Mateo del Sauz and Don Cristóbal Ramírez de Arellano and a party of 150 to 200 men northward to search for Piachi and hopefully find a source of food.

After an exhausting trek across 40 leagues of difficult terrain, the party finally came upon some towns along the Alabama River, several small ones and one larger one, called Nanipacana, with about 80 homes. These villages were southwest of where Mabila and Piachi lay on the Alabama River. Initially, the people of Nanipacana fled as Luna's men approached, but they were wheedled back with ribbons and glass beads as gifts.

Back at Polonza, Luna waited anxiously for about 45 days until a small detachment from Sauz arrived to report that the expedition was safe and sound in the town of Nanipacana. They had found a considerable amount of cached corn in the village, and they suggested that the rest of the colonists join them. Luna decided to take this advice, but before anyone could leave, he became sick with a debilitating fever and hallucinations, and all trips were delayed until February.

When his health returned, Luna sent two expeditions to Nanipacana. One rowed two brigantines and two barks to Mobile Bay and then up the Alabama River, while the other went cross-country led by him. When the two parties arrived at Nanipacana, they were shocked to learn that the inhabitants had fled across the river, taking most of their food stores with them and destroying the crops growing in the fields (Hudson et al. 1989). Luna searched all over the area, but everybody had fled.

On April 15, 1560, starving and growing more and more desperate, Luna sent Mateo del Sauz with a party of 40 cavalry and 100 foot soldiers north to Coosa (Hudson 1988). Several soldiers in this group had previously been to Coosa with de Soto and they had along a woman who had been taken captive there and would serve as their translator. Also in the party were two friars, Domingo de la Anunciación and Domingo de Salazar.

Hungry and traveling in unfamiliar terrain, del Sauz and his detachment made their way very slowly. On June 10, they reached the town of Onachiqui in northern Alabama, where, for the first time, the local people did not flee and even supplied them with burden-bearers. The Sauz party then crept slowly from village to village eating all the food they could find. Hudson (1988, 604) suggests that "for the poor Indians, these Spaniards must have been like locusts, eating everything in their path."

After Onachiqui they came upon Apica, on the upper Coosa River, and then Ulibahali at present-day Rome, Georgia, another important town visited by de Soto in 1540. The people of Ulibahali were initially friendly but became so appalled at the voracious appetite of the Spaniards, that they devised a scheme to get rid of their guests. As de la Anunciación described:

> One day after the sun had gone down, an Indian arrived at Ulibahali, to judge from his appearance and demeanor, seemed to be a chief; he was accompanied by four other Indians. He carried the emblem of an ambassador, and he stated that he was such, and came from the great providence of Coza. He carried in his hand a cane of six palmos in length [a palmo is 8 inches], adorned at the top with white feathers, which appeared to be those of a heron. It was the custom of the Indians to emphasize their messages of peace by wearing white feathers and their declaration of war with red ones. When the ambassador arrived within sight of the Spaniards, he made his obeisance after his fashion and said that the head of Coza had sent him in the name of the whole province, offering it to them and thanking them in advance for their inclination to use it and entreating them that his desires to receive them should not remain unfulfilled and that they should hurry to go there as he offered them those who would guide them and serve them [Swanton 1922, 255–56].

Del Sauz and his group were delighted by this news but, not wanting to leave a reliable food source so soon, told the ambassador to go on ahead and they would follow later. The ambassador claimed that he was ordered to accompany them, and the Coosa expected them very soon. The Spanish reluctantly left the next day, and the "ambassador" absconded as soon as they were well on the road.

The Spanish Arrive at Coosa

The group reached the main town of Coosa on July 26, just as a new crop of green corn and beans was ready to harvest. There were seven small settlements around the main town, scattered along a 10-mile stretch of the Coosawattee River. The area was by no means as bountiful as they had been led to believe from the previous expeditions. La Anunciación related:

The whole province was called Coza [Coosa], taking its name from the most famous city within its boundaries. It was God's will that they should soon get within sight of that place which had been so far-famed and so much thought about and, yet, it did not have above thirty houses or a few more. There were seven little hamlets in its district, five of them smaller and two larger than Coza itself, which name prevailed for the fame it had enjoyed in its antiquity. It looked so much worse to the Spaniards for having been depicted so grandly, and they had thought it to be so much better. Its inhabitants had been said to be innumerable, the site itself as being wider and more level than Mexico, the springs had been said to be many and of very clear water, food plentiful and gold and silver in abundance, which, without judging rashly, was that which the Spaniards desired most. Truly the land was fertile, but it lacked cultivation. There was much forest but little fruit because, as it was not cultivated, the land was all unimproved and full of thistles and weeds. Those they had brought along as guides, being people who had been there before, declared that they must have been bewitched when this country seemed to them so rich and populated as they had stated ... [However,] those from Coza received the guests well, liberally, and with kindness, and the Spaniards appreciated this, the more as the actions of their predecessors did not call for it [Swanton 1922, 231].

The Spanish recorded much about the Coosa and their villages.

Their dress is what nature gave them, except that the women wear girdles of thread from mulberry roots; they arc about two palms wide and with them, they cover their privy parts. They all live together in little towns, for so far we have seen none which contains as many as one hundred and fifty houses, and very few which number above forty or fifty. They have winter and summer houses. The winter houses are all covered with earth, and they sow whatever they like over them. All the towns have a good-sized plaza outside the town, in which there is a pole like the "rollo" of Spain; they are very tall, and they have them for their sports. There are some towns enclosed by a pair of walls as high as a man's stature [Priestley 1928, 239].

The Coosa Feed the Spanish

To obtain food, Luna's men were conciliatory and appeasing to the locals rather than displaying the aggressiveness of the previous de Soto group. They traded ribbons and colored beads for food rather than just taking it. They camped on the outskirts of villages and tried not to disrupt the lifeways of the locals. They posted sentinels at night to protect their encampment from the Coosa and keep their men from messing with the local women. "The Spaniards were afraid that the Indians of

Coosa would rise up against them or that they would simply leave, taking their supplies of food with them" (Hudson 1988, 609).

The Coosa did not give the Spanish unlimited access to their food; instead, they brought daily rations to the Spanish camp. Each man and horse were given about an ear of corn a day, and some beans and pumpkins. The Spanish camp was provided with about six bushels a day.

> The people of this land of Coosa seem to us to be more peaceful and to confide in us more than all those we have left behind, though they are not so confident as to neglect to put their property and women in safety while they wait for us in their towns with a few serving women and bring us food to our quarters. Ordinarily, we camp somewhat apart from the towns lest the horses or any uncontrolled persons injure the cornfields or raise a commotion among the inhabitants. They do not give us food in as great abundance as our need requires, but we think best to preserve the peace by suffering a little want rather than to bring on war by seeking abundance [Priestley 1928, 237].

It was not a lot of food, but it was a godsend for the hungry Spanish. La Anunciación exulted, "Lord, there is no lack of food, nor do we even expect to lack it" (Priestley 1928, 223).

Coosa Farming Methods

The way the Indigenous people grew their crops was a surprise to the Spanish. Instead of clearing large areas for that purpose as they did in Spain, the Coosa only opened small holes in the forest, providing just enough food for a year. La Anunciación felt that this situation did not suit well the Spanish plans for colonization:

> As to making a settlement, it appears to us that the country is not as well suited for it as we thought. It seems very densely forested, and in as much as the Indians have the good part of it occupied, if a settlement were to be made, it would be imperative to take their lands from them. So for this reason and for others, it is desirable that you come and send orders as to what is to be done. For even though the natives have been observed to be so disposed of that they can be utilized profitably, the country is so poor and with such scant opportunities for gainful pursuits that we think it would be difficult to maintain ourselves [Priestley 1928, 223].
>
> All the towns that there are in this country are on the banks of the rivers, for all the rest is so densely wooded that it can by no means be inhabited; this, we think, is the reason there are so few people in this county, for even those who are here have very limited tracts of land; except that which is

cleared around the towns, all the rest is claimed by the forest. The principal reason why we left Narupacana was, as said above, to search for a site possessing the conditions which his Majesty and you in his royal name command. There must be from Coosa where we now are, to Nanipacana where we started, one hundred and twenty or one hundred and thirty leagues, and in all of this, we have seen no location where a settlement of Spaniards could be made, even though we might be willing to turn the natives out of their houses, for the reason that the cleared land is so scant that it does not even suffice for the natives themselves. So that no cattle of any kind can be raised here to the owner's profit, without which and other sources of gain that this country lacks your Lordship may readily see how—the Spanish people could [not] live [Priestley 1928, 241].

The Coosa Ask for Help

After the Spanish had been in Coosa for about two weeks, some of the principal men visited del Sauz and asked him if they would help them in their war with the Napochi.

As la Anunciación recalled, they asked:

> Sir, we are ashamed not to be able to serve you better, and as we would wish, but this is only because we are afflicted with wars and trouble with some Indians who are our neighbors and are called Napochies. Those have always been our tributaries acknowledging the nobility of our superiors, but a few years ago they rebelled and stopped their tribute and they killed our relatives and friends.... Now, it seems only reasonable, that you, who have so much knowledge, should favor and increase ours. Thou, Senor, hast given us thy word when thou knowest our wish to help us if we should need thy assistance against our enemies. This promise we, thy servants, beg of thee humbly now to fulfill and we promise to gather the greatest army of our men [people], and with thy good order and efforts helping us, we can assure our victory. And when once reinstated in our former rights, we can serve thee ever so much better [Swanton 1922, 232].

The Napochi were once a tributary society of the Coosa that had become hostile and were blocking some of their critical northern trade routes. Subsequent to their contact with de Soto, the Coosa population had diminished greatly in size, while the Napochi had become more numerous, perhaps swelling in size after taking in refugees from the de Soto warfare. They also may have been less touched by European diseases.

Hudson et al. (1989, 43) suggest:

Six—The Luna Colony and the Coosa

It is clear that the Southeast seen by the members of the Luna expedition was undergoing rapid change following the De Soto expedition. These changes would in time fundamentally alter the complexion of the Southeast as the once powerful chiefdoms collapsed (DePratter 1991). Such a collapse was no doubt accelerated by the presence of the Luna expedition itself.

Del Sauz consented to the Coosa request, offering them 25 cavalry and 25 infantrymen.

> The Indians got together almost three hundred archers, very skillful and certain in the use of that arm, in which, the fact that it is the only one they have has afforded them remarkable training. Every Indian uses a bow as tall as his body; the string is not made of hemp but of animal nerve sinew well twisted and tanned. They all use a quiver full of arrows made of long, thin, and very straight rods, the points of which are of flint, cut in triangular form, the wings very sharp and mostly dipped in some very poisonous and deadly substance. They also use three or four feathers tied on their arrows to ensure straight flying, and they are so skilled in shooting them that they can hit a flying bird. The force of the flint arrowheads is such that at a moderate distance they can pierce a coat of mail [Swanton 1922, 233].

The Coosa marched in eight different groups, and each had a captain, carrying a stave that was 12 feet long, with white plumes waving at its top. Del Sauz provided a horse "fixed with all the trappings" to carry the Coosa chief dramatically in the rear guard. An African slave was ordered to guide the animal since the chief had never ridden before.

The Coosa and Spanish marched all day hungry, as both groups assumed the other would bring food.

At the end of their first day of travel

> eight Indians, who appeared to be chiefs, entered the camp of the Spaniards, running and without uttering a word; they also passed the Indian camp and, arriving, at the rearguard where their cacique was, took him down from his horse, and the one who seemed to be the highest in rank among the eight, put him on his shoulders, and the others caught him, both by his feet and arms, and they ran with great impetuosity back the same way they had come. These runners emitted very loud howling, continuing them as long as their breath lasted, and when their wind gave out they barked like big dogs until they had recovered it in order to continue the howls and prolonged shouts. The Spaniards, though tired from the sun and hungry, observing the ceremonious superstitions of the Indians, upon seeing and hearing the mad music with which they honored their lord, could not contain their laughter in spite of their sufferings [Swanton 1922, 234].

The Coosa continued to run, carrying their chief about a half-league from the camp, where there was an elevated area that was five meters high, with steps leading up to it. This was likely a mound from an abandoned town that had once belonged to the Coosa. The paramount chief then climbed up to the top of the mound,

> and he began to speak to them, admonishing the whole army to be brave, restore the glory of their ancestors, and avenge the injuries they had received. "Not one of you," he said, "can help considering as particularly this enterprise, besides being that of all in common." Remember your relatives and you will see that not one among you has been exempt from mourning those who have been killed at the hands of the Napochies. Renew the dominion of your ancestors and detest the audacity of the tributaries who have tried to violate it. If we came alone, we might be obliged to see the loss of life, but not of our honor: how much more now, that we have in our company the brave and vigorous Spaniards, sons of the sun and relatives of the gods.... None of you can think that this action is not particularly yours, in addition to its being an action on behalf of all of you. Remember your relatives, and you will realize that not one of you has been exempt from mourning those who have been killed by the Napochies. Renew the lordship of your ancestors and detest the impudence of the tributaries who have tried to violate it. [Swanton 1922, 235].

At the end of their second day of travel, they discovered their first Napochi village and camped beside it. When they attacked it at first light the next morning, they found that the inhabitants had all fled. The Spaniards and Coosa made chase and soon came to a second Napochi village along the bank of the Tennessee River. When the Coosa and Spaniards began crossing the river, these Napochi also began to flee, but the Coosa overtook them. Trapped and outnumbered, the Napochi sued for peace and agreed to again become dutiful tributaries of the Coosa. The Spaniards then appropriated a large quantity of corn from the Napochi and headed back home with the victors.

Polonza Is Abandoned

When del Sauz arrived back at Coosa in late June, he learned that Luna and the remaining colonists had abandoned Nanipacana and gone back to Polonza on the coastline. It turned out that when Luna had gotten word that del Sauz had arrived in Coosa, he had ordered all the colonists to move into the interior, but they had refused. "His colonists who had become recalcitrant and complaining, now became positively mutinous" (Hudson 1988, 622).

Not long after the raid of the Napochi, del Sauz and his detachment followed Luna back to Polonza, as he had been ordered to return if they didn't find the interior suitable for colonization. The Coosa at least feigned sadness that the Spanish were leaving and gave them what supplies they could to support them on the road. Several Coosa accompanied the Spaniards on the trail for the first couple of days. Del Sauz and his detachment arrived at Polonza in early December.

The wretched, starving, and querulous colony at Polonza staggered on for another three months, with Luna repeatedly lashing out at everyone. Finally, on Holy Thursday, Ángel de Villafañe arrived with food and relief and assumed authority as governor of both La Florida and Punta de Santa Elena. Luna departed on the first boat that sailed to Havana, and Villafañe began to remove the rest of the colonists who had survived (Hudson 1988).

Incredibly, Villafañe's first major action was to leave 50 men at Polonza and sail with the rest of the colony (about 230) to Santa Elena. After attempting several landings on the coast of Georgia while looking for a suitable port, the fleet was hit by a hurricane and Villafañe was forced to flee to Hispaniola and then Havana. Here most of the soldiers and colonists scattered. After three months in Cuba, Villafañe returned to Polonza, removed the remaining 50 colonists, and took them to Mexico. This ended the Spanish attempt to settle the Gulf Coast.

Seven

Jean Ribault and the French Attempt to Settle Florida

1562–1565

Setting the Stage: The Huguenots' Search for a Safety Valve

The Huguenots were a religious group of French Protestants, mainly nobles, educated tradesmen, and military officers, who practiced the reformed, or Calvinist, tradition of Protestantism. "Huguenot numbers grew rapidly between 1555 and 1561 in France, and by 1562, the number of them was approximately two million, concentrated mainly in the western, southern, and some central parts of France" ("Huguenots" 2022). There were about 16 million Catholics in the country at that time.

When Henry II died in 1559, his sickly 16-year-old son succeeded him as King Francis II. He was married to sixteen-year-old Mary, Queen of Scots, who had been his childhood friend since she had arrived at the French court at the age of five. During the 18 months of Francis II's reign, Mary pushed him to persecute French Huguenots on charges of heresy and have them tortured and burned as punishment.

When Francis II died in 1561, Mary returned to Scotland and the pressure against the Huguenots was relieved. Ten-year-old Charles IX was made king, with his mother Catherine de' Medici as regent (Probasco 2017). In that year, the royal Edict of Orléans ended the persecution of Huguenots, and in 1562, the Edict of Saint-Germain formally guaranteed them freedom of conscience and private worship. The

SEVEN—Jean Ribault and the French Attempt to Settle Florida

tension between the Protestants and Catholics smoldered for decades, however, erupting into eight civil wars between 1562 and 1598.

In 1562, the admiral of France, Gaspard Coligny de Châtillon, a leader of the early French Protestant movement, commissioned Jean Ribault to lead a mission to Florida to find a place where Huguenots could settle, away from the tensions of France. This colony was hoped to be "a safety valve in relieving Huguenot political pressure on France's Catholic government, pressure strong enough at that moment to threaten civil war" (Harris 1963).

France would be the first European country to challenge the Spanish colonial claims on Florida. The French were very aware of the legend of Chicora propagated by the early Spanish explorers, and they targeted the southern low country of South Carolina as the site for their colony. What followed was a long saga of disappointment, bloodshed, and failure, recorded in four published narratives: Jean Ribault's own *The Whole & True Discouerye of Terra Florida* (1582); his second-in-command René Goulaine de Laudonnière's *L'histoire notable de la Floride* (1586); *Brevis narratio eorum quae in Florida* (1591) by artist Jacques Le Moyne de Morgues; and *Discours de l'histoire de la Floride* (1566) by Nicolas Le Challeux, a carpenter on the 1565 expedition. For quotations I have used the English translations of Connor (1927) for Ribault, Bennett (1975) for Laudonnière, and Perkins (1875) for Le Moyne.

Who Was Jean Ribault?

In the mid–sixteenth century, Jean Ribault (also spelled Ribaut) was one of France's most accomplished seamen. A native of the port city of Dieppe, Ribault had sailed with Norman merchant fleets in European waters from his teenage years. For much of the 1540s and 1550s, Ribault lived in England, working with Sebastian Cabot in the English Admiralty, gathering military intelligence for both France and England. He played a key role when France recaptured Calais from England in 1558 and in 1559 had ably watched over French interests in Scotland.

As described by his translator Jeannette Thurber Connor:

> Ribaut had two obligations and inspirations in life: his persecuted Huguenot faith; and his French patriotism, one of the noblest things in this world. Ribaut possessed eloquence, magnetism, great influence over his subordinates, the proverbial Norman shrewdness and that strong and bracing

education of the sixteenth century ... which, while it laid stress on bodily exercises, also developed the faculties of the mind [Ribault 1927, 3].

Ribault Heads to La Florida

Ribault was given a small force of two ships and about 150 men. His target area was to be northern Florida/southeastern Georgia, just outside of most of the Spanish activity.

On April 30, 73 days out from France, Ribault and crew sighted the first land somewhere near St. Augustine, Florida. A pinnace was sent out to search for a place to land but returned a few hours later after finding no harbor nearby. Ribault continued north along the coast and, as evening began to fall, spotted with "unspeakable pleasure" what appeared to be "a leaping and a breaking of the water, as a stream falling out of

Ribault's arrival at the mouth of the St. Johns River. Jacques Le Moyne de Morgues and Theodor de Bry, "Gallorum Praefectus columnam, in qua Regis Galliarum insignia, statuit" (1591); *Le Moyne Plates*, Image 6 (Digital Commons at the University of South Florida).

the lands into the sea" (Ribault 1927, 66). The next morning, he noted, they "entered into a goodly and great river [the St. Johns River], which ... [they] found to increase still in-depth and largeness, boiling and roaring through the multitude of all kinds of fish" (Ribault 1927, 66).

As they entered the river, Ribault "perceived a great number of inhabitants there, coming along the sands and sea links," approaching the Frenchmen "without any taking of fear or doubt," showing them "the easiest landing place" (Ribault 1927, 66). The people who came to them were "all naked and of a goodly stature, mighty, faire and as well shapen and proportioned of body as any people in all the world, very gentle, curious and of a good nature" (Ribault 1927, 29). The women and children were hesitant, but soon people began to arrive in great numbers, bringing evergreen boughs for the chief and his visitors to sit on as they tried to communicate. These Indigenous people were the Saturiwa, a Timucua society surrounding the mouth of the St. Johns River in Florida.

First Timucua—French Encounters

Ribault spent two days at the mouth of the St. Johns River, planting a stone column to stake out France's claim and replenishing the ship's water and stores. Groups on either side of the river did what they could to aid the visitors, bringing them everything a hungry sailor might want, including fish, oysters, crabs, lobsters, beans, maize, and fresh water.

Ribault reported that they had

> entered and viewed the country thereabouts, which is the fairest, most fruitful, and pleasantest of all the world, abounding in honey, venison, wild fowl, forests, woods of all sorts, Palm trees, Cypress and Cedars ... also the fairest vines in all the world, with grapes according, which without man's help or trimming will grow to tops of Oakes and other trees that be of wonderful greatness and height. And the sight of the fair meadows is a pleasure not able to be expressed with the tongue: full of curlews, bitterns, mallards, woodcocks, and all other kinds of small birds [Ribault 1927, 72].

In one of the first European accounts of Indigenous agriculture, Ribault also observed:

> About their houses, they labor and till the ground, sowing their fields with a grain called Maize, whereof they make their meal: and in their Gardens

they plant gourds, cucumbers, Citrons, peas, and many other fruits and roots unknown to us. Their spades and mattocks are made of wood, so well and fitly as is possible: which they make with certain stones, oyster shells, and muscles, wherewith also they make their bows and small lances: and cut and polish all sorts of wood that they employ about their buildings [Ribault 1927, 73–74].

Ribault Continues North

Ribault then headed up the coast of Georgia, naming the rivers he passed after those he knew from Europe. Around the middle of May, as the ships headed towards today's southern South Carolina border they were hit by a massive storm that separated the ships from their pinnaces working along the shore. When the storm was over, the pinnaces discovered they were in a harbor that Ribault described as "exceeding the others in size and beauty" (Ribault 1927, 23).

His second-in-command Laudonnière wrote in his account:

> We lowered sails and dropped anchor in ten fathoms of water. The depth of the water is so great there, where the sea begins to flow, that the largest ships of France, yes the galleons of Venice, could enter there [Laudonnière 1975, 23].

They cast anchor, and the captain and the soldiers went ashore:

> [We] found a place so pleasant that it was beyond comparison. It was completely covered with numerous tall oaks and cedars, and underneath them there were gums of such good aroma that they alone would have made the place most attractive. Strolling under the branches, we saw many turkeys flying through the forest, and some red and grey partridges, somewhat different from ours, chiefly in their large size. We also observed deer running through the woods, and some bears, wolves, panthers, and many other types of animals not known to us. Being pleased with this place, we went fishing there with our seine and took an unusually large number of fish [Laudonnière 1975, 23].

They also had their first encounter with the local Guale people, who at first ran into the woods and hid and had to be encouraged to show themselves. Ribault wrote:

> At first they were in doubt about our intentions and were fearful, but later on they were reassured. The captain showed them certain trading merchandise, and from this, they could understand that he meant them no harm [Ribault 1927, 26].

Seven—Jean Ribault and the French Attempt to Settle Florida

Ribault Settles at Port Royal

Ribault named the harbor "Port Royal" and deemed it to be the place where the French should settle. The location was on present-day Parris Island, South Carolina. Ribault planted a second stone column there and asked for two dozen volunteers to stay behind while he returned to France for reinforcements. So many men were willing to remain that he was forced to choose. Ribault and his soldiers then built a fort he christened "Charlesfort" after their king, provisioned it with food and ammunition, and on June 11 headed for home. He promised he would come back in six months.

Ribault returned to a country embroiled in a civil war. The Huguenots of Dieppe were under attack by the Catholic forces of the government, and after fighting with his townsmen, Ribault was forced to flee to England. There he tried to get Queen Elizabeth interested in supporting his colony but wound up in the Tower of London imprisoned on suspicion of being a spy. He wrote his account of his voyage to America while incarcerated there.

The Fate of the First Colonists

For a while, the colony prospered in the bounteous area that Ribault had selected, but the colonists proved inept at provisioning for themselves, neglected to plant any crops, and came to rely totally on the Indigenous people for their food. As Laudonnière writes:

> After they had been there for a short time, the food began to run short. This forced them to go to their neighbors for assistance in their necessities. The neighbors gave them part of everything they had, except the seed grain they needed for sowing their fields [Laudonnière 1975, 42].

As time wore on, the food stocks of the local people also began to run low, and the colonists had to go deeper and deeper into the woods to forage for food. To make matters worse, a fire broke out in the fort that destroyed most of the Frenchmen's remaining supplies.

The colonists also suffered under poor leadership. Ribault had left Charlesfort under the command of an experienced soldier, Albert de la Pierria, but he proved to be a cruel disciplinarian. He had one colonist hanged and another banished to a nearby island for relatively minor offenses. When he refused to provide that man with food, the garrison rebelled and executed him.

Now, without a leader and out of supplies, the colonists decided they must build a ship and return home. Only one man, Guillaume Rouffi, felt he had a better chance of survival if he stayed behind.

The men of Charlesfort were as clueless about boat building as farming. They did the best they could, however, with the help of now-friendly local people who were likely very happy to see them go. The colonists used whatever materials they could scavenge. Pine resin and Spanish moss were used to caulk the seams of the boat, and old clothing and bed sheets were sewn together to make sails.

From the beginning, the trip out to sea was a disaster. Soon after they embarked, the sea became so calm that they progressed less than 100 miles over a period of three weeks. Now realizing that they faced a very long trip, they began to tightly ration their food at 12 grains of maize per day for each. Soon all the maize was consumed, and they resorted to eating their shoes and leather coats for food. Their fresh water ran dry, making them drink seawater—and some even their own urine. The boat also began to leak so badly that they had to continually bail to keep it from sinking. To add to their misery, they were hit by a powerful storm, which increased the leaking and badly damaged one side of the boat.

Things got so bad that the men gave up and quit bailing, deciding it would be better just to drown. However, one resolute man convinced them that land could not be more than three days away, and they struggled on. After that three days had come and gone, and still without sight of land, the men began dying of starvation. In despair, with nothing left aboard to eat, they did the unthinkable. As Laudonnière recorded:

> So, in this last despair, some of them proposed that it would be better that one die than that all should perish. They agreed that one should die to sustain the others. The one who was executed was Lachere. His flesh was equally divided among his companions, a thing so pitiful to recite that my pen is loath to write about it [Laudonnière 1975, 50].

At this grim point, they finally sighted land and were intercepted by an English ship. Remarkably, it carried a Frenchman from Ribault's original company. He recognized his former crew mates despite their pitiful state and made sure that they were well treated.

Seven—Jean Ribault and the French Attempt to Settle Florida

The Spanish Destroy Charlesfort

When Philip II of Spain learned that the French had sent an expedition to La Florida, he protested mightily to the French government about this threat to Spanish territorial claims. The French completely ignored his complaints, and, in 1563, frustrated, King Philip ordered the governor of Cuba, Hernando de Manrique de Rojas, to find and destroy the French settlement.

De Rojas set off in early 1564, located the now abandoned settlement of Charlesfort, burned it to the ground, and captured Guillaume Rouffi, who had been the sole French representative in North America for a little over a year.

Under grilling from de Rojas, Rouffi described how the French had vacated Florida with help from the locals. According to him: "Seeing that Captain Jean Ribaut did not come nor did any other Frenchmen, [the settlers] decided to go away to France and for that purpose built a twenty-ton boat near the fort; that when it was finished the Indians of the country gave them a number of ropes made of the strong bark of trees and they rigged the boat with these." The Guale also gave them supplies and some blankets that they made into sails for the boat. Rouffi stayed behind, "realizing that there would not be in the boat anyone who understood navigation" (Wenhold 1956, 58).

Laudonnière and the French Return

Despite the horrific experience of the original colonists, the Huguenots still viewed America as a possible haven. In 1564, while Ribault was still imprisoned in England, protestant leaders tapped Ribault's original second-in-command, René Goulaine de Laudonnière, to lead a new mission. Laudonnière departed on April 22 from Le Havre commanding three ships and 300 people, including 110 sailors, 120 soldiers, and, as Le Moyne described:

> a number of nobles, youths of ancient families, drawn only by the desire of viewing foreign countries; for they asked no pay, volunteering for the expedition at their own cost and charges [Perkins 1875, 3].

Most of these would prove to be averse to any real work.

Laudonnière arrived at the mouth of the St. Johns River on June 22,

1564, the place he had previously visited with Ribault before they settled at Port Royal. He and 12 men went on a reconnaissance mission and met up with a group of 400 Saturiwa, who greeted them warmly. They showed them a shrine that they had built around the monument left behind by Ribault two years earlier. Laudonnière wrote:

> Then the chief suggested going to see the stone column that we had erected during the voyage of Jean Ribault, and of which I have already spoken. It was a thing to which they ascribed great significance. Having granted their request to go to the place where the stone was set up, we found it to be crowned with magnolia garlands, and at its foot there were little baskets of corn which they called in their language "tapaga tapola." They kissed the stone on their arrival with great reverence and asked us to do the same. As a matter of friendship, we could not refuse [Laudonnière 1975, 61].

Laudonnière decided to establish his colony here rather than travel further north to Port Royal. He built a fort, named it Fort Caroline, and sent his ships back to France for more supplies and additional colonists.

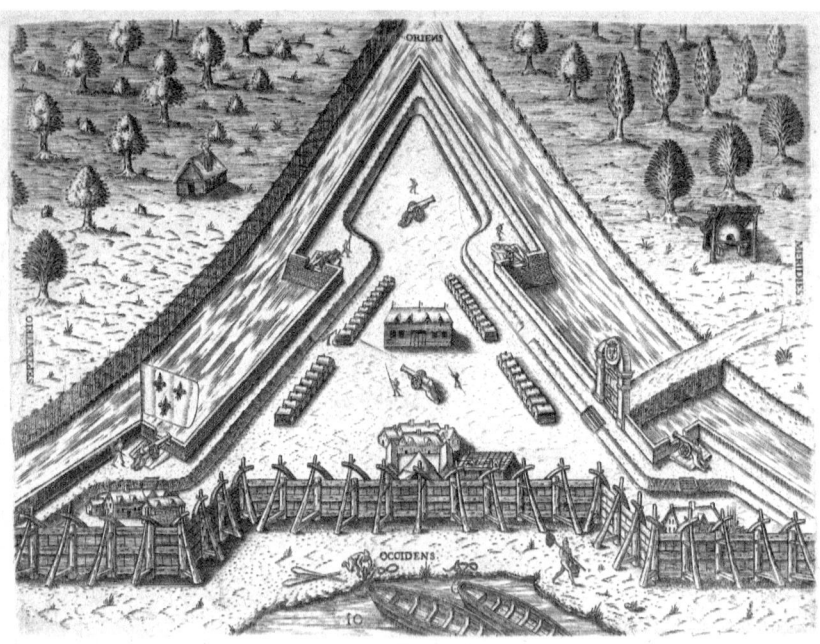

Fort Caroline in an etching of Jacques Le Moyne de Morgues and Theodor de Bry, "Arcis Carolinae delineatio" (1591); *Le Moyne Plates*, Image 10 (Digital Commons at the University of South Florida).

Seven—Jean Ribault and the French Attempt to Settle Florida

The settlers established a flour mill, a blacksmith, and a bakery, and they began regular religious services.

Expeditions were sent out to search for gold, to no avail, although the Timucua traded them a few gold and copper items. What the settlers didn't prioritize, as usual, was the planting of crops. The dependence of the colony on resupply by ships from France (and the Indigenous people) would again become their fatal error.

About this time, the local chief Saturiwa sent messengers to Laudonnière asking for help in attacking his enemies upriver, the chiefdom of Utina. Le Moyne wrote:

> Laudonnière gave an ambiguous reply to these ambassadors; for we had learned, in the course of an extended voyage up the main stream of the River of May [St. John's River], that the enemy of our neighbor King Saturioua [Saturiwa]was far more powerful than he; and that, moreover, his friendship was indispensable to us for the reason that the road to the Apalatcy Mountains (which we were desirous of reaching because we were informed that most of the gold and silver which we had received in trade) lay through his dominion.... Laudonnière had been sending out men to explore the remoter parts of the country, more particularly those in the vicinity of the great King Outina [Utina], the enemy of our own neighbor, and from whom, by the channel of some of our Frenchmen who had got into relations with him, a good deal of gold and silver had been sent to the fort, as well as pearls, and other valuable articles. But this duty was not allotted to everybody; and, as those employed on it were supposed to be growing rich very fast, many began to be envious of them; and, although M. de Laudonnière promised that everything should be distributed equally to all, many were dissatisfied [Perkins 1875, 6].

In late August 1564, Saturiwa decided he would have to campaign against Utina by himself since Laudonnière was now clearly reaching out to his enemy. The spurned chief then successfully attacked an enemy settlement and took two hostages. Upon his return, Laudonnière, still trying to curry favor with Utina, forced him to return the hostages. This was an "ill-considered action": "Saturiwa, greatly irritated by this act of bravado, began to consider all the means possible to avenge himself" (Boucher 2018, 150).

For a while, Laudonnière remained focused on Utina and his presumed gold. He sent several arquebusiers to aid Utina in an attack on his rival Potano, and several of the colonists moved into his village. However, the rapport between the French and their new best friend, Utina, did not last long (Boucher 2018). Laudonnière became convinced that there was gold in the "Apalatcy Mountains" west of Utina's domain, and he began negotiations with another chief, Hostaqua, who lived near those mountains.

Pierre Gambié, the First Trader to Live Among the Amerindians

One of the first Frenchmen to live with the Indigenous people of North America was Pierre Gambié, who settled among the Timucua in a village on the Rivière de Mai (St. Johns River). Taking advantage of his developing language skills and his possession of trade goods from France, he was able to befriend a tribal chief and marry his daughter. He became a de facto leader during the absence of the chief and "treated the chief's own men so tyrannically that ... in the end [he] made himself hated by all of them" (Perkins 1875, 10).

Sometime in 1564–65, Pierre Gambié was murdered as he traveled from the Florida interior to Fort Caroline, laden with trade goods. One of the two guides ferrying Gambié split open his skull with an axe and then made off with his riches. Revenge may have played a role, as Gambié's murderer had been beaten by the Frenchman during a tirade in the Timucua village. Le Moyne suggested that when the man found himself paddling behind his oppressor, he "came to the conclusion that such an opportunity for revenge and plunder was not to be missed" (Perkins 1875, 10).

Settlement Affairs Under Laudonnière

From almost the start, Laudonnière had great difficulty managing the colony; the settlers who were not soldiers resented his rigorous military rule, and he played favorites among the nobles. He also was stricken with a fever, probably malaria, which greatly diminished his strength.

As described by Le Moyne:

> But by this time the noblemen who had come from France to the New World from ambitious motives only, and with splendid outfits, began to be greatly dissatisfied at finding that they realized none of the advantages which they had imagined, and promised themselves; and complaints began daily to be made by many of them. On the other part, M. de Laudonnière

Seven—Jean Ribault and the French Attempt to Settle Florida

> himself, who was a man too easily influenced by others, evidently fell into the hands of three or four parasites and treated with contempt the soldiers, who were just those whom he should have most considered. And, what is far worse, indignation began to be felt by many who professed the desire to live according to the doctrine of the reformed gospel, for they found themselves without a minister of God's word [Perkins 1875, 5–6].

No crops were planted, and the men spent most of their energy searching for silver and gold. Food stocks fell low, and soon after the fort was built Laudonnière was forced to deeply ration.

> Laudonnière proceeded to shorten the allowance of food and drink: so that, after three weeks, only one glass of spirit and water, half and half, was given out daily per man, and as for provisions, which it had been hoped would be abundant in this New World, none at all were found; and, unless the natives had furnished us from their own stores from day to day, some of us must assuredly have perished from starvation, especially such as did not know how to use firearms in hunting [Perkins 1875, 5].

Similar to the previous situation at Charlesfort, Laudonnière's colony had come to rely too heavily on Timucua's generosity for their sustenance. When winter came, and the neighboring nation's food stores also became exhausted, they became reluctant to trade. As Le Moyne tells it:

> The Indians, after a time, began to be slow in bringing in supplies, because they found that most of us had no longer anything to give for them; and it is not unknown to you that these savages do not give anything without getting something for it. When after this they found that no commodities at all were forthcoming from any of us, and when the soldiers undertook to extort supplies from them by blows (as some of them began to do, to the great grief of the wiser among them), they deserted the whole neighborhood; so that we lost even those sources of supply which we had, and even with the continued aid of which we had nothing better to expect than the extremity of hunger [Perkins 1875, 7].

All the Frenchmen could do was forage for acorns and roots to keep from starving. They twice attacked villages of the local chieftain's rivals to seize surplus corn. Some desperate soldiers even raided what had been friendly Timucua villages, poisoning relations.

In the spring of 1565, Utina had finally had enough and totally rebuffed a request for food. In response, the French took him hostage and tried to ransom him back for maize. This high-handed approach led to an unprecedented crisis. On July 27, 1565, a group of colonists traveled into Utina's territory hoping to secure food, and they were ambushed by hundreds of Timucua warriors. In a day-long battle, two Frenchmen were killed and 22 wounded. At this point, relations between the French and Timucua reached "rock bottom," and "the settlers, surrounded by hostile Indians, became virtual prisoners in their own fort" (Boucher 1918, 152).

Laudonnière lamented in his journal that the French difficulties were not his fault and instead were due to the lack of support from home.

> We had endured so many hardships and deprivations in order to explore it, only to lose it through the default of our own countrymen. If we had been re-enforced at the time and place promised, the war which we had with Outina would not have occurred and we would not have antagonized the Indians. I had taken such pains to bind them to us by good friendship [Laudonnière 1975, 141].

A Mutiny

As conditions worsened, Laudonnière was forced to put down several attempted mutinies. In the most serious one, a group of more than 30 colonists met in an assembly and presented to Laudonnière a litany of demands:

> Those present most urgently beseech you to cause the third of the ships which brought us from France, now lying in the river, to be repaired and fitted out; to man her with such persons as you may see fit; and to send her to New Spain, which is not far from this province, to obtain supplies by purchase or otherwise; not doubting that this measure will relieve us [Perkins 1875, 9].

Laudonnière refused, and that night he was taken from his bed at knifepoint, confined in chains, and imprisoned. He was not released until he relented and

> authorized the greater part of his force, in consequence of the scarcity of provisions, to proceed to New Spain to obtain supplies, and requesting all governors, captains, and others holding any office under the king of Spain, to aid them in this business [Perkins 1875, 9].

A group of the conspirators then sailed to the Gulf of Mexico, but instead of bringing supplies back to the colony, they became pirates and wreaked havoc in Cuba. As Le Moyne tells it:

Seven—Jean Ribault and the French Attempt to Settle Florida

> They then fitted out the two shallops that were before mentioned, taking the requisite armament and provisions from the king's stores, and selected the pilots and crews for the voyage to New Spain.... They went to Cuba, where they captured some vessels, in some cases with little difficulty, and laden with supplies of all kinds, such as cassava, olive oil, and Spanish wine; and they took possession of these ships for their own purposes, leaving their own vessels. Not content with this booty, they made descents upon several points on the island, carrying off enough plunder, as they reckoned, to come to two thousand crowns apiece. Afterward, they took, though not until after a fight; a swift vessel with great wealth on board, and with her the governor of a certain port on that island called La Havana. This official offered a great sum of money as a ransom for himself and his two children [Perkins 1875, 9].

Eventually, the French pirates' luck ran out.

> Our ferocious Frenchmen found themselves beset by two large men-of-war, whose broadsides were ready to be opened upon them on either side, and another large vessel besides. Finding themselves thus trapped, as the entrance to the harbor where they lay was narrow, they were greatly cast down; but six and twenty of them threw themselves into a small fast-sailing vessel that was in the place, as she was less likely to be hit by the balls; and, cutting her cable, fought their way out through the enemy. All the rest, however, who remained on board the ship with the governor, were taken, and, except five or six who were killed in the affair, were carried off to the mainland, and thrown into prison [Perkins 1875, 14].

Those who escaped had no provisions and having nowhere else to go went back to Georgia and the St. John's River, where they hoped they could get supplies from friendly local people. Their presence was soon discovered by the garrison, however, and they were captured and condemned, the ring leaders put to death.

John Hawkins Comes to the Rescue

The starving colonists now begged Laudonnière to build a ship large enough to sail across the ocean so that they could return home. As Le Moyne tells it:

> Some of us had actually perished of hunger, and all the rest were starved until our skin cleaved to our bones, M. de Laudonnière, at last, gave up hopes of receiving reinforcements from France, for which he had now been waiting eighteen months, and called a general council to deliberate on the means of returning to France. It was herein finally concluded to refit as well

as possible the third of our ships, and to raise her sides with a plank so as to enlarge her capacity; and, while the artificers were employed on this work, the soldiers were set to collect provisions along the coast [Perkins 1875, 15].

While the group was busily employed in refurbishing the ship, an unexpected visitor appeared on their shore, to their great relief:

> A certain English commander named Hawkins, who was returning home from a long voyage, came up to their fort in his boat; and, on observing our miserable condition, offered us any assistance in his power, and proceeded at once to make his offers good, for he sold to M. de Laudonnière one of his ships at a very moderate price, together with some casks of flour which we baked into biscuits. He also gave us several casks of beans and peas and accepted as part payment in advance some of our brass cannon, and then proceeded on his voyage [Perkins 1875, 15].

Queen Elizabeth's famous sea dog John Hawkins was returning from selling 400 African slaves in Venezuela, and after being blown to the Caribbean on his way home, he had gone on the shore near Fort Caroline for water, only to find the colonists in desperate straits.

Hawkins and crew were surprised at the sad state of the colonists. The voyage's chronicler, John Sparke "the younger," noted:

> Had not God sent us thither for their succor; for they had not above ten days of victuals left before we came. In which perplexity our captain seeing them, spared them out of his ship twenty barrels of meal, and four pipes of beans, with diverse other victuals and necessaries which he might conveniently spare: and to help them the better homewards, whither they were bound before our coming, at their request we spared them one of our barks of fifty ton. Notwithstanding the great want that the Frenchmen had, the ground doth yield victuals sufficient if they would have taken pains to get the same; but they being soldiers, desired to live by the sweat of other men's brows.... Maize was the greatest lack they had because they had no laborers to sow the same [Burrage 1906, 124].

They were forced to rob and steal because they would not grow their own.

New Sails in the Harbor

While the relieved settlers were waiting for a favorable wind to return home, incredibly, another group of sails was seen on the horizon. Jean Ribault had finally arrived in relief with eight ships and 600 more settlers and soldiers. As Le Moyne remembered:

SEVEN—Jean Ribault and the French Attempt to Settle Florida

This arrival, so wholly unexpected, filled us all with joy. M. de Ribaud landed with a number of his officers and many gentlemen and others. They all thanked God, while they were administering to our necessities, that they found us alive, for they had been informed that we had all perished; and so, after the long affliction which we had endured, God sent us happiness. All the newcomers individually were liberal in imparting food and whatever else they had brought and tried in every way to be serviceable each to such friends or kinsmen or fellow countrymen as he met with among us: so all the place was filled with happiness. But this joy was brief, as we quickly found [Perkins 1875, 16].

The euphoria over Ribault's return would soon be dashed, as another much more sinister fleet followed Ribault into the mouth of the St. Johns River. It was led by Pedro Menéndez de Avilés, who had been sent by King Philip with about one thousand soldiers and settlers to uphold Spain's long-standing claim to Florida. Menéndez's arrival was, in fact, no surprise to Ribault, who had been sent to repulse an expected attack. Over the next few weeks, with the torment of a hurricane, Ribault's soldiers would be routed, the French colony destroyed, and most of its occupants massacred.

Lifeways of the Timucua and Guale

Timucua

The Timucua people lived in central Florida, in an area encompassing nearly 20,000 square miles, with an average density of more than 10 people per square mile (Milanich 1996). Their territory stretched from the Altamaha River and Cumberland Island, south to Lake George, and from the Atlantic Ocean to the Aucilla River in the panhandle.

There were about 35 Timucua chiefdoms, each containing two to 10 villages that were divided into family clans (children belonged to their mother's clan). The largest and best-known of the eastern Timucua groups were the Mocama, which were composed of two major chiefdoms, the Saturiwa and the Tacatacuru (Deagan 1978). The Saturiwa population center was around the mouth of the St. Johns River where the French landed, and their main village was on the river's south bank. Further south of the Saturiwa was the Utina, who lived along the river from about the Palatka area south to Lake George. The area between these two groups was largely unpopulated, serving as a barrier between the two peoples, who were frequently at war.

The Timucua lived in the northeast and north-central portions of Florida, and probably numbered overall between 200,000 and 300,000 people organized in a number of chiefdoms. They were seminomadic and, in the fall and winter, planted maize, beans, squash, melons, tobacco, and various root crops, employing slash-and-burn techniques in the inland forests. They collected wild fruits and berries, and baked bread from the root starch of the cycad coontie plant, *Zamia integrifolia*. They also hunted wild game, including deer, alligator, bear, and turkey. In the hot summer, they migrated to the cooler seashore, where they fished and collected oysters and shellfish.

Villages of the Timucua were generally near lakes or streams, and individual houses were palm-thatched with dome-shaped roofs and inhabited by nuclear families. There were also public granaries or storehouses and council houses. Village chiefs were selected from the dominant clans, as well as lesser officials. The chiefs could extract tribute from the villagers and require them to work the fields under his control.

The Timucua played several musical instruments, including flutes of shell or wood and gourd rattles. Before entering battles, priests and shamans were consulted and led ceremonies where a special tea was drunk, made of the cassina plant (*Ilex vomitoria*). The priests and shamans also conducted religious ceremonies and acted as healers. They cured with certain herbs, prayers, and ritual fires.

The techniques used by the Timucua for hunting and fishing included deerskin disguises, fire drives, fish weirs, spears, snares, and bows and arrows. They manufactured baskets and fired clay vessels of many forms, including bowls. Gourds and wood containers were used. They cooked and smoked meat and fish on wooden frames over a fire; boiled fish, meat, and nuts in water; and ground corn in wooden log mortars to make corn fritters.

The Timucua were very tall:

> Spanish explorers were shocked at the size of the Timucua, well built and standing four to six inches or more above them. Perhaps adding to their perceived height was the fact that Timucuan men would wear their hair in a bun on top of their heads. All were heavily tattooed, and such tattoos were gained by deeds usually in hunting or war ["Timucuan: Original Florida natives" 2018].

Seven—Jean Ribault and the French Attempt to Settle Florida

The Timucua worshipped the sun and the moon, and the chief held the most religious power, although shamans played an important role in daily lives. Shamans were involved in almost every part of life, from planting crops to helping women give birth. Shamans predicted the future, cursed people, controlled the weather, performed blessings, and cured people. They used native plants around them to cure people with illnesses.

Guale

The Guale were found along the coast of present-day Georgia and the Sea Islands, north of the Altamaha River and south of the Savannah River (Saunders 2000). They lived in the low country salt marshes.

The Guale lived in semipermanent settlements. They built Mississippian-type platform mounds, which were used for ceremonial, religious, and burial purposes. The largest mounds had council houses on top. While the elite lived in ceremonial centers with mounds, most of the Guale lived in large, scattered settlements (26,000 to 55,740 square meters) along the marsh edge.

The Guale were organized politically into paired chiefdoms, having two coequal towns (Jones 1978). They were a matrilineal society, in which power and privilege were conferred through the female line. A boy's uncle's social standing was more important to him than his father's. At the most important villages, the paramount chief lived with the other important members of his lineage and their families, including his brothers and other male relatives related to him through his mother. The smaller villages under his control were generally administered by one of his brothers or nephews.

The chiefs led by consensus, and all decisions were made by the principal men. Laudonnière observed:

> The men do nothing without assembling and counseling together thoroughly before arriving at a decision. They meet together every morning in the great public house where the king is and where he sits on a seat higher than all the others [Laudonnière 1975, 14].

Tribute was paid to the elite, and "much of this was redistributed down the hierarchy" (Saunders 2000, 31). Elite men could be polygynous, keeping each wife in a separate house.

Houses were built using wall trenches or individually set posts, with a central fire pit. The major supports were of yellow pine, and the walls were constructed of clay daub tempered with Spanish moss. The two sexes worked separately—the men hunted, and the women did the housework. Their diet emphasized estuarine resources and deer, but native plants and cultivated maize also played an important role.

Not much is known about the crafts and tools made by the Guale. Saunders (2000, 38) suggests:

> Our appreciation of the Guale and their predecessors as artisans is limited because only their inorganic artifacts have been preserved. Even direct references to Guale crafts are rare in the documents. However, documents do indicate a rich craft inventory for coastal natives in general; one that the Guale might be expected to share.

Eight

Pedro Menéndez de Avilés Takes Charge of Florida
1565–1566

Setting the Stage: The Threat of the Privateers

None of the sixteenth-century Spanish explorers had found any real wealth in their forays into North America, including Ponce de León, Lucas Vázquez de Ayllón, Pánfilo de Narváez, Hernando de Soto, and Tristán de Luna. The promise of Atlantic America had fallen far short of the glitter of Mexico and Peru. Regardless, King Philip II of Spain still felt that Florida was an important possession, if only to protect his treasure fleets passing through the Straits of Florida.

Of particular concern to the Spanish was that the French Huguenots would violate their New World territories through colonization. As was described in the last chapter, this is exactly what happened in 1565, when Jean Ribault and René de Laudonnière established colonies in South Carolina and Florida.

The king was greatly alarmed by the French presence in the American Southeast, as their corsairs had already been wreaking havoc throughout the Florida Straits. Between 1536 and 1568, 152 ships were captured by French and English privateers in the Caribbean region, and 37 traveling between Spain, the Canary Islands, and the Azores (Durand-Gasselin). "In the 1550s, predation by French pirates had cut in half the Spanish royal revenue from the New World" (Taylor 2001, 76).

In 1564, Pedro Menéndez de Avilés was commissioned by Phillip II to find and remove any intruders who were not subjects of the Spanish crown, explore the coast of eastern North America from the Florida Keys to Canada, and establish permanent colonies for the defense of the Spanish treasure fleet. Menéndez also hoped to find his son, Admiral Juan Menéndez, who had disappeared off the coast of South Carolina in a hurricane.

Menéndez expected to make huge profits for himself and his family in this Florida enterprise, through the development of agriculture, fisheries, and trade. He was backed by a kinship alliance of 17 families from northern Spain that were tied together by blood relations and marriage. They were willing to support his venture in hopes of becoming rich themselves through large land grants and military offices.

Who Was Pedro Menéndez de Avilés?

When Pedro Menéndez was sent to Florida, he was already well known as one of the ablest Spanish conquistadors, and it was natural that he be sent there by his king to set up settlements to protect Spanish interests. Born into the landed gentry, Menéndez was commissioned by Charles V in 1549 to drive pirates from the coasts of Spain, and five years later he was made captain of the Indies fleet. Menéndez was responsible for identifying where the major royal fortresses would be built across the Caribbean and would be the architect of the great Armada de la Carrera, which carried the riches of Spanish America back to Spain. Menéndez charted the route they followed, which led through the Florida Strait and along the east coast of Florida, to ride the Gulf Stream.

Menéndez was a man of action who spent as little time as possible on administrative details and made many enemies. In fact, he was imprisoned in 1563 by the Casa de Contratación, along with his brother Bartolomé, accused of accepting bribes and smuggling silver. However, he was released two years later by the king, who needed his considerable talents to purge Florida of the French and protect his treasure fleets.

The First Expedition of Menéndez to Florida

We are fortunate to have multiple Spanish and French reports on the first Menéndez expedition. His brother-in-law Gonzalo Solís de Merás recorded the most complete Spanish account—*Menéndez de Avilés y la Florida: Crónicas de sus expediciones*. French versions of the

EIGHT—*Pedro Menéndez de Avilés Takes Charge of Florida*

Pedro Menéndez de Avilés by José Camarón y Boronat (1730–1803), published by Francisco de Paula Marti in 1791 (Georgetown University Art Collection / Wikimedia Commons).

events can be found in René Goulaine de Laudonnière's *L'histoire notable de la Floride* (1586), Jacques Le Moyne de Morgues's *Brevis narratio eorum quae in Florida* (1591), and Nicolas Le Challeux's *Discours de l'histoire de la Floride* (1566). In this chapter, I quote Laudonnière from Charles Bennett's 1975 English translation, *Three Voyages*. For quotes from the journal of Solís de Merás, I use Arbesú's 2017 translation: *Pedro Menéndez de Avilés and the Conquest of Florida: A New Manuscript*.

Menéndez set sail from Cádiz on July 28, 1565, in the *San Pelayo*, along with several smaller ships, and briefly anchored at a place he called San Agustin (today's St. Augustine), named after the Catholic feast day. Nearby was the Timucua village of Seloy, home to probably 200 people.

Menéndez then proceeded north to the St. Johns River basin, where he found the French settlement. He entered the harbor, and, as Solís de Merás recalls, referring to Menéndez as the Adelantado (military and civil governor):

> When they came close to the French fleet, about eleven thirty at night, the enemy began firing artillery, but the balls passed through the masts and rigging of the Adelantado's ships without doing any harm. He did not consent to any artillery being fired from his ships but rather commanded that on all his vessels—all the soldiers should go below in order not to be insured … commanded the trumpets to hail the enemy, and they responded, hailing him with their own.
>
> After these salutes were over, the Adelantado spoke to them courteously, saying to those on the flagship: Gentlemen, where is this fleet from? One of them said it was from France.
>
> He went on to say: What is it doing here? They replied: We bring infantry, artillery, and supplies for a fort which the King of France has in this land, and for others, he is yet to build.
>
> The Adelantado said to them: Are you Catholics or Lutherans? And who is your general? They replied that they were all Lutherans of the new religion, and their general was Jean Ribaut. They then ask who they were, who was the man asking them questions, whose fleet that was, why had it come to this land and sea and who was its general.
>
> The Adelantado replied: He who asks this of you is called Pedro Menéndez, this fleet belongs to the King of Spain, and I am its general. I have come here to hang and behead all the Lutherans I may find on this land and sea. These are the instructions from my King, which I will fulfill when the day comes, for I will board your ships, and if I find any Catholics, I will treat them kindly.
>
> Many replied at once with various insults and abusive words against our lord the King and against the Adelantado [Solís de Merás 2017, 45–46].

Menéndez and crew then tried to board the enemy ships, but the French cut the cables, hoisted their sails, and fled. The adelantado made chase until dawn without success and at 10 the next morning headed

EIGHT—Pedro Menéndez de Avilés Takes Charge of Florida

back towards St. Augustine to regroup. There, Menéndez disembarked his troops, formally claimed Florida, and built fortifications in anticipation of a French attack. The chaplain of the expedition, Father Francisco López de Mendoza Grajales, celebrated the first mass in North America.

Ten days after Menéndez left, Ribault decided to try to demolish the Spanish forces before they got a foothold and set out on a preemptive strike, with his four largest ships and most of the soldiers. He left Laudonnière in the fort with scanty support. In his journal, Laudonnière would lament:

> Of those who remained from my company, there were sixteen or seventeen who could bear arms, but they were all convalescent and sick. The rest were wounded and crippled persons, recovering from the battle which my lieutenant had made against Outina [Laudonnière 1975, 163].

As he searched for Menéndez, Ribault was caught in a hurricane and blown off course. While Ribault's fleet was struggling, Menéndez sent his troops overland in driving rain to attack Fort Caroline. They easily overwhelmed the lightly defended garrison and slaughtered 140 male colonists, sparing only 60 women and children.

Only 50 were able to flee the attack, including Laudonnière, Le Moyne, and Le Challeux. They managed to get to the coast, where Ribault's son Jacques was anchored with five of the smaller ships that had not been part of the chase. After a heated debate, the survivors decided to scuttle the three smallest vessels and make haste back to France in the two remaining ships.

Meanwhile, Jean Ribault's fleet floundered in the hurricane and was driven south towards present-day Daytona Beach. All the ships were smashed along the rocky shore, and Ribault and about 400 other survivors were washed ashore. According to Laudonnière's account, those who made it to land regrouped and walked together north towards Fort Caroline. A Spanish patrol came upon these tattered remnants of the French force and took most of them prisoner. Only a few were able to run away, to take their chances with the local Timucua rather than hope for Spanish mercy. The captives were given the opportunity to repent their Protestant ways, but most refused. The unrepentant were taken behind a sand dune and slaughtered, then mutilated in a fury of anti–Protestant religious zeal.

In the published eyewitness accounts of the Spanish, far fewer people were executed, and they were murdered over a more protracted period. John McGrath (1997) suggests that there were two different massacres, occurring about two weeks apart. In the first, about 140 men stranded on a sandbar were confronted and executed by Menéndez, except for of about two dozen who were either Catholic or possessed valuable skills.

> In the second encounter, Ribault, leading some two hundred survivors from his grounded flagship *Trinite*, offered to surrender if Menéndez would promise to spare his men. Menéndez refused. As a result, fewer than half of the Frenchmen surrendered while the rest fled into the woods.... Again, Menéndez chose to execute his prisoners, whose deaths at that point still accounted for only a fraction of the total forces of the French fleet [McGrath 1997, 22].

Regardless of how these events transpired, the annihilation of the French forces and settlers from Fort Caroline signaled the end of any significant French presence in southeastern North America. Almost all their subsequent activities in the Southeast would be privateering. The French would now focus most of their energy to the north in predominantly Canada, following a trail blazed by Jacques Cartier.

The Timucua's Involvement in the French Defeat

Timucua played a significant role in the battles between the Spanish and French. And in fact, "Menéndez's timely arrival gave the locals an opportunity to settle the score with the disruptive settlers" (Boucher 2018, 147).

The Timucua played several key roles in the defeat of the French. First, the residents of Seloy offered no resistance when Menéndez established his base of operations in their territory. In fact, the chief gave the Spaniards a large house located by the riverbank, allowing them to quickly store any goods that could be affected by the rain. The Timucua also provided Menéndez with critical geographic information about La Caroline and the surrounding area. The locals directed the Spanish fleet to the fort, which was hidden a few leagues down the river and described the best route for an attack. They led them on their cross-country trek in the driving rain to the fort and kept the Spanish abreast of French activities in the fort. They told them when Ribault went to sea and how weak the garrison was after he left. In addition, "following the fall of La Caroline, the Timucuans drove the final nail in the Huguenot coffin by providing critical intelligence regarding the whereabouts of French survivors" (Boucher 2018, 164).

Menéndez Settles In

After destroying the French settlement, Menéndez headed back to St. Augustine with 200 soldiers, leaving behind the rest of his men at the captured fort, which he renamed San Mateo. He named his brother Bartolomé governor of the district of St. Augustine, extending from San Mateo to the Mosquito River. The expedition's chaplain, Father Francisco López, established the first mission on North American soil, Nombre de Dios, to serve the local Timucuan villages.

From the beginning of his occupation, it became abundantly clear to Menéndez that he couldn't conquer the overwhelmingly large populations of Indigenous people, and for his fledgling colonies to survive, he would have to learn to coexist with the Timucua. It was critical that he was perceived as a friend and not an adversary, something that the French had failed to accomplish. This would prove to be a tricky road. As Eugene Lyon (1976, 118) put it:

> The Spanish invaders never had sufficient numbers to affect a real invasion, particularly where the French already had a degree of influence with the Indians and the native cultures were well organized.... Menéndez sought to implant Spanish settlements alongside the Indian cultures without disturbing their essential rights on the land. He did not endeavor to change at once their religious and political arrangements. Wherever he went in Florida, the adelantado proclaimed the overlordship of Philip II as the rightful ruler of the land and sought to make arrangements with the Indians based upon this concept.

Menéndez had not been in St. Augustine very long when he received the disturbing news that there was still a potential pocket of French resistance in Florida that needed to be extinguished. As Woodbury Lowery (1911, 215) tells it:

> Three weeks had barely passed after the final massacre when word was brought by the Indians that the seventy or eighty Frenchmen belonging to Ribaut's company, who had refused to surrender, were constructing a fort thirty leagues distant from St. Augustine in the neighborhood of Cape Canaveral ... and were also building a vessel which they intended to send to France for assistance. Again, Menéndez determined to act promptly.

From Ponce de León to Sir Walter Raleigh

On August 23, Menéndez sent two forces to root out the French—one a group of 100 men that went by sea in three light boats and another one of 150 that marched with him across the land, guided by Timucua. The Spaniards converged on the fort on November 4, approaching it by land and sea. Upon seeing them, the French hurriedly escaped into the forest, and Menéndez had their ship and fort burned.

It did not take the French very long to realize that they had to surrender, and this time, Menéndez decided to treat them kindly, feeding and clothing them. He had much greater resources at his disposal than before. The group of Spanish and French then marched about 45 miles along the coast south, to an Indigenous Ais village, where the ships linked up with them.

The local Ais cacique received the group with warmth, kissing their leaders on the mouth. As Lowery describes the scene (1911, 2017):

> His face was decorated with various colors, and he as well as all of his chief men wore frontlets of gold, probably obtained from the vessels wrecked along the coast. Menéndez ordered his men to respect the property of the natives and presented them with little gifts of knives and mirrors and scissors.

The group remained for four days at Ais before moving on about nine miles further to a lagoon in the vicinity of Cape Canaveral, which was teeming with fish. There Menéndez built another fortress and left Captain Juan Vélez de Medrano as the local governor, along with 200 of his men and the 50 French prisoners. He hoped isolating his settlement from the tribal village would reduce conflict with the Ais.

Menéndez then sailed to Havana to get supplies, taking with him 50 of his men and 20 French prisoners in two small, open boats and leaving the others with enough supplies for 15 days.

The trip to Havana was, according to Lowery (1911, 218–19), "a bold and dangerous undertaking."

> Impelled only by the wind and by oars in the hands of weary and famishing men, he had to stem the swift-flowing currents of the Gulf Stream, which reaches its greatest velocity in this neighborhood. He had observed in his previous journeys the existence of back currents along the Florida shore, and availing himself of these, he followed down the coast, discovering on his way the two inlets at Gilbert's Bar and Jupiter, and in three days reached Cuba. During the crossing, a storm arose, and Menéndez shared the tiller with one of the Frenchmen. On leaving Ays, his compass had been broken, and missing Havana during the night, he made the harbor of Bayahonda,

fifteen leagues beyond ... and he shortly reached Havana, where he was joyfully received by Diego de Amaya, the commander of the second boat, who had arrived two days before giving him up for lost.

Relief Ships to Florida

After a bout with illness, Menéndez focused his energies on obtaining and providing sustenance to his Florida forts. He sent Diego de Amaya from Cuba to St. Augustine and San Mateo with supplies of sea biscuits, meat, cassava, corn, and some cattle. When Amaya arrived at St. Augustine, he discovered that more than 100 of the colonists had died, the survivors were almost naked, and they were suffering greatly from the cold. Discontent was percolating throughout the settlement, and many were speaking ill of the country and wanted to abandon it. Amaya was able to resupply St. Augustine, but not San Mateo, as his ship was destroyed in a gale, and he was forced to return to Havana on another ship.

Upon his return, Amaya headed to the garrison at San Mateo, but he had difficulty finding it. Eventually, he sighted a small boat carrying the leader of the colony, Captain Juan Vélez de Madrano, just south of the St. Lucie Inlet. Vélez told him "a harrowing tale of hardship and mutiny":

> Soon after the departure of the Adelantado, the previous November, the garrison's rations had given out. The friendly Indians possessed no store of food sufficient for such a large body of men. As discipline disintegrated, bands of soldiers roamed the area seeking food. Friction between the Indians and the Spanish became an outright war. A soldier named Escobar persuaded one hundred of his fellows to desert and to march southward with him seeking an escape from Florida and passage to New Spain [Lyon 1976, 140].

Amaya and the captain then joined forces and sailed along the coast, looking for a more promising site for a colony. They found one at Jupiter Inlet, and there, on December 13, 1566, they built a new fort they christened Fort Santa Lucía. Amaya then headed back to Havana to report to Menéndez, while Vélez went off to recover his rebel soldiers.

Menéndez Visits the Calusa

On February 10, 1566, Menéndez decided it was time to search for any surviving castaways along the Gulf Coast of Florida. Between

1520 and 1564 at least 12 Spanish ships had been destroyed along the coast besides his son's (Reilly 1981). Menéndez had gotten word of a Calusa cacique named Carlos who supposedly held some Christian captives.

Menéndez discovered his first castaway on February 18 near present-day Fort Myers. Here, when he went on shore, he was greeted by a Spaniard named Hernando de Escalante Fontaneda, who had lived among the Calusa from 1549 to 1566. Fontaneda told Menéndez that more than 200 shipwrecked Spaniards had been captured by the Calusa over the last 20 years, and while most had been sacrificed, a few were still alive.

The Calusa had made a fortune on the recovery of shipwrecked goods, as Allender (2018, 825) relates:

> Throughout the 16th century, Spanish ships were wrecked on the Florida coast year after year and often multiple times a year, providing the Indians with a wide array and regular supply of European materials of every description ... the Calusa recovered immense quantities of goods directly from ships lost in the immediate vicinity and indirectly through the payment of tribute by native groups living on the central and south Florida Atlantic coasts and in the Florida Keys.

Menéndez anchored his ships and sent Fontaneda to alert the Calusa cacique that he had come to trade. What Menéndez had stumbled upon was the capital of the Calusa empire, a village of about one thousand people on an island, later known as "Mound Key" in Estero Bay near present-day Fort Myers. On this island today, one can still find a series of high mounds, with a central temple mound that is 31 feet in height and has a 50-foot-wide canal that bisects the island southwest to northeast.

Soon after Menéndez had landed, Carlos appeared with about 300 Indian archers, hoping to rout the Spaniards, as they had done with Ponce. Menéndez ordered the ships' artillery to the landward side of the ships and disembarked with 30 arquebusiers to meet Carlos. The two leaders quickly concluded that the situation was a standoff and that it made much more sense to trade gifts rather than to fight. Menéndez gave Carlos a shirt, a pair of silk breeches, a doublet, a hat, and some other gifts for his wives. In return, Carlos presented Menéndez with a bar of silver.

Menéndez then suggested that if Carlos and his lieutenants would come on board his ship, he would feed them and give them more gifts.

EIGHT—Pedro Menéndez de Avilés Takes Charge of Florida

He hoped that once he had them on board, he could ransom them for any shipwrecked sailors being held in Carlos's village.

As Solís de Merás tells the story, Menéndez told Carlos "that if he and his principal Indians were to board the ships, he would give them and their wives many things to eat."

> The chieftain did so, driven by greed, and took about 20 Indians with him. With great secrecy and diligence, the Adelantado ordered each soldier to place himself next to an Indian and not letting them throw themselves overboard if they were to attempt it. He ordered the cables with which the brigantines were moored to be played out and stood offshore....
>
> The chieftain wanted to leave, but the Adelantado told him that his lord, King of Spain, had sent him for the Christian men and women he had there and that if he refused to release them, he would have him killed, he begged him to give them up, for he would give him many things in exchange and he would be his great friend and brother. The chief said he was satisfied, and he would fetch them.... The chieftain did so out of fear, and within an hour, they brought five women and three Christian men, to whom the Adelantado had shirts given.... All this time, the Christians were weeping for joy, which was a sight to behold [Solís de Merás 2017, 89–90].

Carlos also promised to give up another three captives that were being held elsewhere and invited the Spaniards to visit his village the next day and share his hospitality.

When Menéndez set off the following day, he was prepared for festivities, taking along gifts, food, and a small band. He also went well-armed in case he had to fight his way back to the ships, taking 200 arquebusiers with him. At Carlos's village, they found hundreds of Calusa gathered in a great house. The adelantado stationed his arquebusiers outside in readiness for trouble and entered the hall with about 20 of his men.

As the celebration began, Carlos called Menéndez his brother and offered his sister to him as a wife. He asked that he take her to the land of Christians, where she was anxious to go. Carlos seated Menéndez in the great house on a raised platform with himself and another woman whom the Spaniard took to be the cacique's wife. Before them, there were about 50 men and 50 women seated on each side. Carlos then went "through a certain ceremony which is like kissing the King's hand here; no greater mark of deference can be given among them, and it is that which Indian vassals are in the habit of giving to their caciques" (Solís de Merás 2017, 92). All the other men and women in the great hall did the same. Outside the window, more than 500 young Calusa girls began to sing, and boys around them began to jump up and down and spin. The men and women seated inside next to Carlos also began to sing.

After a great feast, as Menéndez got up to go, Carlos sprang his own trap.

> The chieftain told him that since he had given him his sister as a wife, he should go to a room nearby and rest with her, and if he did not, his Indians would be outraged, claiming that they and she were being mocked and that he did not value her much.... The Adelantado showed a little perturbation and told him that Christian men could not sleep with non–Christian women. The chieftain replied that since he had already taken him for his elder brother, he and his people were already Christians [Solís de Merás 2017, 95].

Menéndez told him that it was not that simple and then launched into a lengthy explanation of the precepts of Christianity and what one must do to become a Christian. Carlos's sister replied that even if he would not take her as his wife, she wanted to return with him to the Christian lands to learn of their religion.

Once back on the ship, the officers debated mightily as to whether Menéndez should take Carlos's sister as his wife. Menéndez was not at all enthusiastic but consented in hopes of building a stronger relationship with Carlos. Menéndez had the woman baptized and given the name Doña Antonia (after St. Anthony), and that evening the marriage was consummated. The next morning, Menéndez informed his new wife that he planned to send her to Havana for instruction in Catholicism while he continued to explore Florida. He promised Doña that he would bring her back in three or four months.

The following day Carlos and other Indians came to see Doña Antonia off. Menéndez received them warmly but took the opportunity to urge Carlos to give up his idols.

> He said that he wished a large cross to be set near Carlos's house, that every day in the morning, the men, women, and children should go to kiss and worship it, that they should regard it as their most important idol, and that he should give up all the other idols he had, explaining the reasons. The chieftain said that he would do so but that he could not give up his other idols so soon until his sister and the Indians that accompanied her came back to tell them what they had to do [Solís de Merás 2017, 99].

A cross was then made, and Menéndez had it set up there, and with much pomp he kissed it on his knees, followed by the rest of the Spanish that were there. Then Doña Antonia and the Calusa women did the same, followed by Carlos and his entourage.

The cross was then turned over to the Calusa. A man who would turn out to be Carlos's chief rival, Don Felipe, received the cross and carried it on his shoulders to his canoe. Don Felipe was the cousin and brother-in-law of Carlos and served as the Calusa war chief. It was likely that he pretended reverence to the cross to gain Spanish support (Reilly 1981).

A Failed Mission to Ajacán

On August 1, 1566, Menéndez sent Ensign Pedro de Coronas in command of *La Trinidad* with two Dominican friars to establish a mission in the province of Ajacán (Chesapeake Bay). He had heard rumors that there was a sea lane there that might be the fabled Northwest Passage that led to northern Mexico, the Philippines, and China, and he did not want it to fall into French hands. Unable to go there himself or send a large number of soldiers, he was content for the time being with the founding of a mission (Vigneras 1969).

Among the group sent was Don Luís de Velasco (Paquiquineo), the brother of the chief of Ajacán. Don Luís had been taken to Mexico as a boy five years before and baptized with the viceroy's name. The record of how he got there is unclear, although it is possible that he was picked up by Villafañe in 1561, during his aborted attempt to transfer the Luna colonists from Polonza to Punta de Santa Elena.

The group set off on August 2 from San Mateo and touched down at several locations in the vicinity of Ajacán, but they saw no Amerindians and Don Luís did not recognize any of the places as his homeland (Vigneras 1969). Finally in October, after being battered by a hurricane, the captain aborted the mission and took them all to Spain, where he had dispatches to deliver.

Upon his arrival in Spain, Don Luís settled right in and spent the next four years studying in Sevilla with Jesuits. He "ingratiated himself to such an extent into the goodwill of Philip II that he lived at the royal expense during all of his stay" (Lowery 1911, 360). His story would not end here as he would be recruited by Menéndez for another mission to Ajacán in 1570. This time, he would find his people and participate in a massacre.

NINE

Pedro Menéndez Struggles to Control Florida
1566–1572

Setting the Stage: Trouble on the East Coast

While Menéndez was in the land of Carlos and busy marrying an Indigenous wife, affairs had reached a desperate point in his Florida east coast presidios (Lowery 1911).

At the settlement of Santa Lucia, Menéndez's hope of friendly relations with the Amerindians proved elusive. Many soldiers had been picked off in ambush as they built their fort, and when it was completed, it was assaulted by at least one thousand warriors, who laid siege for over four hours. They shot six thousand arrows into the fort, wounding the captain and killing eight soldiers. The agile Ais were able to shoot 20 arrows for each shot the soldiers got off from their arquebuses. The attacks were renewed daily, and it became impossible for the colonists to go out in search of food. The soldiers were forced to eat anything they could find that was edible—animal bones, shoes, and leather belts—until only 30 men were left who were strong enough to bear arms.

A sub-lieutenant and the vicar Mendoza tried to sail a ship to Havana for succor but were driven back by foul weather. When they got back, the soldiers took over the caravel, wounding Mendoza, and headed out to sea. By this time, rations in the fort had become so pitiful that only 75 of the 250 Spanish soldiers and French prisoners were still alive.

At San Mateo, while some supplies had trickled in from Havana, rations were still woefully insufficient, and widespread fighting had erupted between a group of mutinous soldiers and those loyal to Commander Pedro de Valdés. One hundred and twenty soldiers had hijacked a relief ship and killed a number of Ais, including two principal chiefs. They forced 35 loyal nobles outside the fort, naked and unarmed, who were slaughtered by the Ais in retaliation. Only de Valdés and a handful of supporters were left in the fort, as the mutineers planned to sail their hijacked ship to Santo Domingo.

Menéndez Returns

In early March 1566, Menéndez left the gulf for the east coast of the Florida peninsula to check on the condition of his presidios. He was in for a shock as the desertions and the deaths caused by illness, starvation, and Indian action had cut the original Spanish forces by almost half.

On March 19, as Menéndez approached St. Augustine, his lookouts sighted a southbound caravel, and when he boarded the ship, he found that he had intercepted the shipload of mutineers.

> [Menéndez] at once informed them of the arrival of succor and offered them a general pardon. But their hearts were set upon abandoning the country. They had enlisted in the hope of conquering another El Dorado; they had encountered but hardship and privation, and they were determined to seek their fortunes elsewhere, in Peru or New Spain, where more substantial returns awaited their endeavors than slow starvation on palmetto roots and grasses—Out of the entire company some thirty-five noblemen, who had joined their ranks, accepted the pardon and returned to the fort. The balance sent word that they had not come over to plow and plant, and that they wished to go to the Indies to live like Christians and not to live like beasts in Florida [Lowery 1911, 243].

On the same day that Menéndez reached St. Augustine, his lieutenant Esteban de las Alas also entered the harbor, bringing supplies from Havana, where he had left Doña Antonia and her companions. He also had with him 200 new volunteers from Cuba to refresh the garrisons at St. Augustine and San Mateo and establish new presidios further north. These fresh soldiers arrived just in the nick of time to restore the enterprise of Florida "and supported the start of a new impetus of exploration and colonization" (Lyon 1976, 153).

Menéndez Establishes Santa Elena

On April 1, 1566, Menéndez set sail for the north to establish a new colony, named Santa Elena, near Point Royal Sound where Jean Ribault had built the short-lived Charlesfort. He was accompanied by 150 men, Esteban de las Alas, who was to be the first governor at Santa Elena, and the Frenchman Guillaume Rouffi (whom the Spanish renamed Guillermo Rufín), who had remained behind when the rest of the French had abandoned their original colony.

The settlement of Santa Elena would be the next step in Menéndez's goal of building a series of forts along the south Atlantic coast. He hoped "to protect an empire which, as he envisioned it, would eventually include all the territory from Newfoundland southward to Florida, and from there around the Gulf coast to the Pánuco River in Mexico" (DePratter et. al. 1983, 126). Making a settlement at Santa Elena on the east coast was considered particularly important to impede the French "who might wish to go to this land of Florida to settle in it and take possession" (Lyon 1976, 17).

After three days of travel, the flotilla was confronted by a "naked Christian" and several Amerindian archers in a canoe. The speaker was one of the refugees of Ribault's colony, now living in the village of Guale, on St. Catherines Island. He told them that the local people were housing several French fugitives and were supporting them in a war with their mortal enemies the Crista. He initially forbade Menéndez from visiting the village but, after a spirited discussion with the Guale, allowed Menéndez to set out with a small band of soldiers.

The Spaniards were peacefully received at the village, and Menéndez began his visit by giving the Guale some religious instruction, as was his custom. A cross was set in the ground and the Frenchman was forced to translate the ceremony. Most of what Menéndez presented was standard religious instruction, but he did put the fear of God into the trembling translator by informing the assembled masses that the "true Christian" Spanish had come to kill the "false Christian" Lutherans. The Guale promised to embrace the faith, probably understanding little of the sermon.

Menéndez remained at Guale for four days, instructing the locals in Christianity and trying to restore peace between the warring tribes. He even managed to orchestrate an exchange of hostages.

He then traveled a little further north to Santa Elena and

NINE—Pedro Menéndez Struggles to Control Florida

established his new colony on Parris Island, South Carolina. There he had more friendly relations with the local people and built a fortification of timber and earth, named San Salvador. Esteban de las Alas was left as governor, with 110 men and six pieces of artillery. A few soldiers were also sent among the neighboring tribes to instruct them in the faith.

Menéndez then headed back to Guale with a small party. When he reached the village, the cacique asked him to pray to his Christian God for rain, as they had been suffering from drought for a long period. After first brushing off his request, Menéndez changed his mind and told the cacique that he would do it if he honored the cross that had been erected on his previous visit. Then as Lowery (1911, 250) describes:

> Kneeling down before it, he embraced it and turning to the Spaniard exclaimed: Behold, I am a Christian. This occurred at two o'clock in the afternoon, and half an hour later it began to thunder and lighten and to rain with such violence that it did not cease for twenty-four hours, and extended in a circuit of five leagues. Then the Indians, astounded at the prodigy, came to the house where Avilés was lodged, and casting themselves at his feet, begged him to leave some Christians with them. The General responded by ordering his nephew, Alonzo Menéndez Marques, with four other Spaniards, to remain among them.

Menéndez then headed back to St. Augustine, along a channel between the islands and the coast. He passed many Amerindians along the way, who begged him to give them crosses, having heard about the miracle in Guale.

After Menéndez left, the settlement at Santa Elena had a very rocky start (Lyon 1984). Forty-three soldiers mutinied on June 3, stole a supply vessel, and fled to Cuba. They left behind 28 soldiers and Alas, disarmed and with little food.

Fortunately, relief was swift, when a fleet of royal vessels arrived carrying supplies and Captain Juan Pardo with a 250-man company. Menéndez also sent a plethora of goods from the Antilles and Yucatán. Quite a cornucopia arrived, including foodstuffs (hogs, biscuits, manioc, corn, and salt meat), hardware (tools, cooking utensils, extra pikes, and cords for the crossbows), and even a bronze bell to call the town together (Lyon 1984). The troops unloaded on July 11 and immediately began building a new fort, San Felipe.

Menéndez Relocates St. Augustine

When he arrived at St. Augustine, Menéndez found the settlement to be at war with the local Timucua, who had attacked the fort at night and had set fire to the thatched roof of the magazine with fire arrows. The storehouse had exploded, destroying its contents and killing many soldiers. The Spanish fought desperately, but their cumbersome arquebuses were again no match for the agility of the Amerindians and their rapidly fired arrows. As Lowery (1911, 252) describes it:

> While the soldier was loading his arquebus, they ran into the grasses and thickets and dropped on the ground when they saw the flash. Crawling swiftly through the underbrush and grasses, they rose at another spot than that at which the Spaniard had aimed, and closing upon him delivered another volley of four or five arrows in the time which he took to load. They went about in small skirmishing parties and fought in ambuscade, shooting the men who went to gather seafood and dwarf palmettos, piercing their clothes and coats of mail. When the Spaniards pursued them they ran to the streams and marshes, threw themselves into the water, and, being naked and swimming like fish, crossed to the opposite shore, bearing their bows and arrows aloft in one hand to keep them dry; there they would stand shouting and mocking at the Spaniards, and when the latter withdrew, they swam back, dogging their steps and shooting at them from the underbrush. The Spaniards found that to hold them in check it was necessary to burn their villages, seize their canoes, cut down their plantations, and destroy their fishways.

After hearing of the siege, Menéndez decided to move the fort to a more defensible position on the north end of the barrier island between the mainland and the sea. The colonists toiled frantically on the new fort, in constant fear of an attack from the Timucua, and they finished it 10 days flat. With the new fort completed, Menéndez headed back to Havana to strengthen the supply lines to his colonies and deal with his Amerindian wife and her companions.

While in Havana, Menéndez learned from the king that a new shipment of supplies was headed to St. Augustine to keep the struggling colony afloat for a while longer. Commander Sancho de Arciniega was on the way from Spain with a fleet of 17 ships, carrying 500 sailors, 1,500 reinforcements, and much-needed supplies for the starving colonists. As would be played out repeatedly over the next century, the beleaguered presidio would receive reinforcements and supplies just before its flickering flame was extinguished.

Francisco de Reynoso Visits Carlos

Before he left for Havana, Menéndez directed Captain Francisco de Reynoso to visit Carlos with a company of 30 soldiers and explore the area. He also ordered Reynoso to erect a fort near the village and encourage Carlos to worship the cross he had been given before.

Reynoso's stay with Carlos would be quite contentious. While some Calusa worshiped at the cross, Carlos scoffed at the practice. He plotted on numerous occasions to murder Reynoso only to be foiled by female informants. Carlos continued to receive shipwrecked Spaniards from all along the coast, which he still tortured and killed. The only thing that stopped him from slaughtering the tiny Spanish contingent was that his sister remained in Spanish hands.

Menéndez Reunites with His Indigenous Wife

Upon his return to Havana, Menéndez discovered that five of the Calusa who had traveled with Doña Antonia had died. Fearing that she might also die and destroy relations with Carlos, he decided that he must return her to her brother as soon as possible.

The day after his arrival, Menéndez called on her and found her to be quite despondent. As told by Reilly (1981):

> She told him that she wished that God might kill her, because when they landed the Adelantado had not sent for her to take her to his house, to eat and sleep with him. Thinking quickly, Menéndez replied that Knights of the Order of Santiago such as himself could not sleep with their wives for eight days after their return from an expedition.

Doña Antonia, using her fingers to count, stated that two days had already passed and that in another six days she would go to his house. Menéndez agreed and told her he would take her to visit Carlos the next day.

When he retired that night at a local inn, he was awoken at midnight by Doña Antonia carrying a candle and sure that there was another woman. She begged him to let her curl up in a corner of his bed, pleading that she would not come near him, so that her brother Carlos could be told that they had slept together, and he would not think that Menéndez was laughing at her. Menéndez refused and sent her away with some gifts, including blouses, mirrors, and bead necklaces.

Juan Pardo Searches for Route to New Spain

Before he left for Havana, Mendoza also ordered Juan Pardo to explore the interior and seek a land and water route to New Spain, thus completing the unfinished work of Hernando de Soto. He was also asked to convert as many of the local people to Catholicism as possible (DePratter et al. 1983). In his travels, Pardo would traverse an extensive area lying between the Savannah and the Wateree, and as far north as the Alleghenies. Pardo of course did not find a route to Mexico, as it was much farther away than Menéndez had dreamed, but he did work hard to convert all the local people he could.

> At all of these villages through which he passed, he had assembled the natives and their chiefs and made them a short address, calling upon them to submit to the Pope and the King, to which the Indians had readily assented, in the evident expectation of thus getting rid of him [Lowery 1911, 276].

As Pardo moved from town to town, he commanded the Amerindians to build houses to serve as way stations for future Spanish travelers and had them fill cribs with maize for the travelers' sustenance. He also made them fill sacks with maize for his soldiers to carry along the route.

About 120 miles from Santa Elena, Pardo constructed his first fort at a village called Guiomae, near present-day Wateree, South Carolina, and then headed north until he reached the Savannah River at Cofitachequi, where de Soto had visited and captured the female cacique 25 years before. A few days later he came upon another village called Yssa on one of the northern branches of the Broad, and two days later Joara, at the foot of the Alleghenies. Here he built a fort he named San Juan. At this point the season was well advanced, the mountains were now almost impassable with snow, and on December 1, 1566, he headed back to San Felipe, leaving his sergeant, Hernando Moyano de Morales, in charge of the fort and 30 men.

While Pardo was away, Sergeant Moyano decided to wage his own war against the Indigenous Chisca in the Georgia mountains (DePratter et al. 1983). De Soto had also mentioned Chisca in his travels but didn't report on any battles. In Moyano's first confrontation, he claimed in a letter to Pardo that he killed more than a thousand people and burned 50 huts, with only two of his soldiers being slightly wounded. He then traveled for four days along a mountain trail and claimed that he destroyed another Chisca village, defended by a very high wooden palisade, killing 1,500 Amerindians. After receiving a serious threat from a mountain chief, Moyano was forced to continue westward down the Nolichucky to the French Broad River, and to Chiaha, near Columbus, Georgia, where there was another great palisaded village of three thousand Creeks. Here they built a small fort, San Pedro, near the fortified capital of Chiaha (known as Olamico, a Muskogean word for "chief town") and awaited Pardo's arrival. The locals avoided a confrontation by receiving the soldiers with respect, offering them food and lodging and helping Moyano build his fort.

Pardo's Second Expedition

In late August 1567, Pardo was directed to rejoin Moyano at Chiaha (DePratter et al. 1983). He headed cross-country from Santa Elena following the route he had used previously, and when he reached Fort San Juan, he found it to be under siege by the Indigenous people, who dispersed as soon as he appeared. He then crossed the mountains and passed through a country so beautiful that his companions compared it to Andalucía. At Chiaha, he caught up with Moyano and his soldiers, and they traveled south together to Satapo, a palisaded village located just south of Knoxville. Here they were told that the de Soto expedition had passed through these parts and "the chief claimed to have killed some of them" (DePratter et al. 1983).

Pardo remained at Chiaha for five days before departing for Coosa, described by de Soto's expedition. He spent several days trekking in the foothills of the Great Smoky Mountains before reaching the village of Chalahume in the Little Tennessee Valley, and then Satapo just downstream. There Pardo was told that the Coosa chief was plotting to ambush him, changing course from their friendly relationship with the de Soto and Luna expeditions. Pardo turned back, leaving by a different route than he had arrived and returned to Chiaha, where he strengthened the original fort and built another blockhouse at nearby Cosaque (or Casque). Pardo then returned to Santa Elena, leaving 30 additional soldiers at Chiaha and 13 at Cosaque.

The subsequent history of these outposts is largely unknown. Pardo and associates had built small fortifications at Olamico or Chiaha (Fort San Pedro), Cauchi (Fort San Pablo), Joara (Fort San Juan), Guatari (Fort

Santiago), Canos or Cofitachequi (Fort Santo Tomás), and Orista (Nuestra Señora de Buena Esperanza). Lyon (1976, 204) suggests that "by June 1568, news had already reached the seacoast that many Spanish soldiers had been massacred by Indians at the inland forts." More than 100 years after Pardo's expedition, English settlers in South Carolina were told by locals that there had been Spanish mining activities in the surrounding mountains and that most of the settlers had been killed in an Amerindian attack in 1584 (DePratter et al. 1983).

Menéndez Returns to the Land of Carlos

On March 1, 1566, Menéndez set sail from Havana to Carlos's village with seven vessels and 150 men including his nephew, Pedro Menéndez Márquez; his wife, Doña Antonia; her surviving companions; and the Jesuit missionaries Father Rogel and Brother Francisco de Villareal.

Within two hours of Menéndez's landing ashore, he was greeted by 12 canoes containing Carlos and his brother-in-law Don Felipe. Menéndez presented Doña Antonia to the greeting party in an emotional ceremony and asked Carlos if he was now ready to visit the land of the Christians. After deliberating with Don Felipe, Carlos declined, stating that he could not go because his people might revolt against him while he was gone. Reilly (1981) speculates that Carlos feared his heir apparent, Don Felipe, would take power and that, in their conference, Carlos had tried to convince Don Felipe to go instead of him to Cuba. Carlos had become leery of Don Felipe, as he had been baptized to gain Spanish favor and was very friendly towards Menéndez.

As he looked around, it became abundantly clear to Menéndez that all was not as he'd hoped it would be in the land of Carlos. As Lyon (1976, 177) relates:

> When he arrived at the Indian settlement, he saw at once that the fierce and intractable nature of Chief Carlos and his people had been little affected by all his initiatives towards them. The surface amity that had prevailed when Carlos had given his sister to Menéndez and the release of the Christian captives had largely dissolved. The return of Doña Antonia was not palliative to the situation, for she told her brother that the marriage to Pedro Menéndez was artificial and unfulfilled.

At a meal with Carlos the next day, Menéndez decided to confront him about his not returning any more Christian captives. According to Reilly (1981), in a grand bluff, Menéndez called him a liar and told him that if he did not immediately bring him more castaways, he would decapitate Carlos and all his followers, burn down their village, and reach out to his enemies. Even though Menéndez had only 30 men, the threat worked, and Carlos sent him some more Christians.

The Search for a Trans-Peninsula Route

One of the major reasons that Menéndez had traveled to Carlos's country was to search for a waterway that passed through the Florida peninsula to San Mateo and St. Augustine. Reynoso had been told that it lay in the country of Tocobaga, up the west coast of Florida, 50 miles distant from Carlos.

It turned out that the people of Tocobaga were Carlos's great enemies, and he asked Menéndez to invade the region and destroy their village. Menéndez proposed instead that they make a truce, saying it was his goal as a Catholic to establish peace among all the tribes and that Carlos should feel obliged to do the same. To make sure that Carlos didn't make mischief in his absence, Menéndez invited Carlos to accompany him on the mission.

Menéndez sailed up the coast at night and arrived in the vicinity of Tocobaga just before dawn. Carlos again pleaded that they attack and massacre the village but was dissuaded by Menéndez. To placate Carlos, however, he promised to negotiate the release of some Calusa captives, including one of Carlos's sisters. Then, as Lowery (1911, 279–80) relates:

> An Indian was sent ashore to proclaim in a loud voice the peaceful mission of the visitors, but the frightened savages, awakened in so unexpected a way at the early hour, fled in terror with their wives and children when they beheld the ship drawn up near their village. Tocobaga alone [the chief of the villiage] remained with five or six companions and a woman, and, the day having broken, sent a Christian slave to Avilés to thank him for not having burned his village and slain his people. The man proved to be a Portuguese trader from Avila, in the Province of Algarve, who had been wrecked upon the coast, where all his shipmates had been killed, and himself ultimately reduced to hewing wood and drawing water for Tocobaga, whom he also served in the capacity of a cook.
>
> Still unwilling that Carlos should come in contact with Tocobaga, Avilés went ashore to see the Indian chief, from whom he soon learned that the

native fear of the Christians was not ill-founded, for white men had already visited the locality, and on the refusal of the chiefs to supply them with corn had killed them, and had themselves, in turn, suffered a like fate at the hands of other Christians, who had proved very friendly to the Indians. Avilés then delivered his customary dissertation upon true and false Christians, recapitulated his own pacific intentions, delivered up to Tocobaga those of his subjects whom Carlos had held as prisoners, and ended by receiving the humble submission of the chief.

Four days later more than 1,500 warriors gathered near the village to receive Menéndez. This was way too threatening, and Menéndez asked Tocobaga to dismiss the bulk of them, retaining only the chief men. Solís de Merás relates:

> Once they were assembled, with the Adelantado seated in the most prominent place, Chief Tocobago said to him that he had told the Indian chieftains who were there everything the Adelantado had said, and that, if he truly meant those things, all of them would be happy to take him as their elder brother and become Christians, and to make peace with Carlos, and give him back his people, with [the proviso] that should Carlos wage war on him again, the Adelantado would help him, and that if [Tocobaga] waged war on Carlos, then the Adelantado would help Carlos. [Tocobaga said] that he wanted to make peace with the true Christians, not the false ones, and that he should leave him another captain with thirty Christians to teach him and his chieftains how to be Christians [Solís de Merás 2017, 178].

As to finding the waterway and seeing where it led, it turned out that a river did pass through the adjacent territory of the Macoya, but these people were the enemy of the Tocobaga and had many warriors. Menéndez decided he had too few men to confront such a force and abandoned the search. Menéndez then departed with Carlos, leaving behind Captain García Martínez de Cos and 30 soldiers to educate the Tocobaga in the Christian faith.

When Menéndez got back to the Calusa capital at Mound Key, he had the blockhouse strengthened, added 50 soldiers to the garrison, and built a chapel. He instructed Father Rogel to study the language of the Calusa and teach them about Christian ways. Doña Antonia was left to her own devices, and from that point on Menéndez had little if any contact with her. She would remain with her people for a time, teaching them about the Catholic faith, but eventually she returned to Havana, where she died.

The Ultimate Fate of Carlos and Don Felipe

After Menéndez's forced peace with the Tocobaga, Carlos felt very disgraced and angry and began plotting against the Spanish with even greater fervor than before. Carlos began to harass the outpost under the command of Captain Francisco de Reynoso almost continually. A Calusa party attempted to capture the missionary Father Rogel and sacrifice him to their gods, but failed. The Spanish were now virtually prisoners in their own blockhouse and were afraid to leave without an armed guard.

Finally, between April and early June of 1567, Reynoso had had enough and ordered King Carlos and his closest advisers killed. Felipe was then installed by the Spanish as cacique, but his reign would be short. Many of Felipe's lieutenants were not happy with his close arrangement with the Spanish, and to placate them he directed several attacks against the Spanish. In frustration, Menéndez finally sent his nephew, Pedro Menéndez Márquez, to assassinate Don Felipe. In a stiff fight where Márquez and many of his men were wounded, he beheaded Don Felipe and 20 other Calusa (Reilly 1981).

Menéndez Returns to the East

Menéndez's next stop was Havana, where he put down a budding rebellion, and from there he traveled back to the southeastern coast of Florida and the land of the Tegesta people.

> He entered into a friendly compact with the chief, who gave him his brother and two other Indians to take to Spain. During his stay of four days Brother Francisco was settled there, a cross erected, a blockhouse built, and a company of soldiers was left in charge [Lowery 1911, 283].

Menéndez then traveled to San Mateo, where he found that Gonzalo de Villarroel, whom he had left in charge, was at war with Saturiwa, who had been on good terms with the Spanish. Menéndez found that many warriors and several caciques had been killed in battle, and Villarroel had put 16 of the principal men in chains. Menéndez was greatly distressed by this situation, as his overriding strategy of colonization was dependent on friendly relations. He had scattered his forces all over Florida and South Carolina, in small, isolated groups who could fall easily to concentrated and sustained attacks.

Attempting to defuse the situation, Menéndez tried to arrange a hostage exchange but failed, and in frustration he turned his back on his own strategy of placation and declared that he would have Chief Saturiwa's head. He never got that head, but the Spanish and Saturiwa would skirmish back and forth well into the 1570s.

Ten

Spanish Florida Staggers Toward the Seventeenth Century
1567–1586

Setting the Stage: Menéndez Is Ordered Back to Spain

In the spring of 1567, Menéndez was called back to Spain by the Council of the Indies and would remain there until April 1568. Before he left, he directed a number of new blockhouses to be built at St. Augustine and San Mateo, and he had them fortified with small garrisons.

On May 18, 1567, he set sail from San Felipe and arrived at his hometown of Avilés in late June. He visited his Spanish wife and then headed to Madrid, taking with him six Amerindians in native dress to present to the king. On his arrival at the court, he was surprised to learn that he had been accused of misconduct by the mutineers who had returned before him, but he easily dispelled these accusations.

The king, now fully convinced of his innocence and importance to the realm, bestowed on him the title of captain-general of the West, awarded him 200,000 ducats, and gave him a new fleet of 12 galleons with two thousand soldiers. It would now be his job to protect all the Caribbean and Florida waters under Spanish control from the corsairs.

A French Revenge

Coincidentally while Menéndez was in Spain, a French nobleman named Dominique de Gourgues decided that he would take it upon himself to revenge Menéndez's massacre of the colonists at Fort

Caroline (Lowery 1911). This event was by no means forgotten and still aroused great indignation among Protestants and Roman Catholics alike. The king had sent complaints to the Spanish court, but Menéndez and his associates continued to be honored for the deed and were not punished.

In 1567, Gourgues decided to even the score with the Spanish. He sold everything he owned and borrowed money from his brother Antoine to buy ships and recruit a crew to avenge the deaths of the Protestants in Florida. Even though he was a Catholic himself, he had a long-standing hatred of the Spanish, having been captured by them during the Italian Wars and having served several years in their galleys.

He sailed from France on August 22 with one small and two large vessels. In his force were 100 arquebusiers and 80 sailors. The intent of the mission was held in great secrecy—the soldiers and crew were told they were going to Africa on a slaving mission.

Gourgues followed a circuitous route along the African coast to Cuba, where the real intent of his trip was finally revealed to his men. He then headed through the Straits of Florida to St. Augustine, where the Spanish observed his ships and fired a warning shot. He decided to wait until nightfall to attack and landed on an island near Fort San Mateo, where the Timucuan Tacatacuru lived, a group closely allied with Saturiwa. Gourgues sent an emissary to them who had previously been at Fort Caroline, and he discovered that the tribe held the only survivor of the former French expedition, Pierre Dugré, a youth of 16 at the time. Dugré would become the mission's interpreter.

The cacique readily agreed to join Gourgues in his attack on San Mateo. The French crossed the water in boats, while their allies swam, and they easily took the redoubt on the opposite side of the river. Of 60 occupants, all but 15 were slain. The French and the Tacatacuru then attacked the principal fort at San Mateo, with its 260 soldiers. The Spaniards,

> greatly terrified and altogether unable to discern between the white men and the savages, took flight for the woods, where they found themselves caught between the Indians and the French. In their panic, the fugitives were all mercilessly slaughtered except some fifteen, who were all later hung along with the other captives [Lowery 1911, 330].

The French had thus gained their revenge.

After the bloody attack, Gourgues returned to the port of La

Rochelle on June 6, 1568, where he was received cordially by the governor of Bordeaux but coldly by the king, who feared further rupture with Spain.

The Gourgues incident signaled the end of European presence at San Mateo and was the last contest between Spain and France south of Canada.

Menéndez Chooses Santa Elena as the Capital of Florida

While busy protecting Spain's treasure ships against French and English corsairs and privateers, Pedro Menéndez had not lost sight of his great ambitions for Florida (Lyon 1984). In his grand plan, Santa Elena would be La Florida's primary eastern anchor. Two more cities would be established 200 leagues west and north of it, as Jesuit missions, settled by farmers and guarded by soldiers.

Philip II agreed to the plan and allowed Menéndez to settle 500 colonists. On October 7, 1568, the caravels *Nuestra Señora de la Victoria* and *Nuestra Señora de la Concepción* left Cádiz for the Indies carrying 225 emigrant farmers from the uplands of Old and New Castile. Many were whole families with children.

Pedro Menéndez paid for their passage to Florida, pledged to support them for two years, and provided them with cows, bulls, oxen, sheep, goats, chickens, and grape cuttings (Lyon 1984). In return, they agreed to a land lease, sharecropping with Menéndez. The ships and colonists arrived on August 1, 1569, and soon had built a tidy little village of 40 houses.

Father Juan Rogel Tries to Establish a Mission

Father Juan Rogel and the Jesuits arrived in June and built a small mission with a church and house for him at Escamazu, in Cusabo or Orista territory, five leagues from the city. Father Rogel had scouted the area the previous summer and had decided "that the Orista and other Indians in the area were more tractable, honest, and less inclined to polygamy, sodomy, and incest than those in South Florida" (Lyon 1984, 4).

Rogel immediately tried to get the Orista to settle in a permanent village rather than follow their annual migrations. At first, they appeared to be listening to his teachings, and he even got them to plant some maize, but soon they dispersed into the forest on their annual acorn harvest. Rogel became increasingly frustrated as Amerindian rituals eroded his teachings of Christian doctrine.

By the fall of 1569, conditions had become dire for colonists and friars alike. While the farmers had managed to plant some barley, wheat, grapes, and vegetables, the harvests were insufficient to meet their needs. They were forced to subsist on oysters and what roots and shrubs they could forage. Remarkably, after a Christmas sermon, during which Father Gonzalo del Alamo had preached that a supply ship from heaven was entering the bar, one did in fact arrive, but their hardships were far from over (Lyon 1984).

In the spring, the commander of Fort San Felipe ordered the surrounding caciques to supply the soldiers with several canoe loads of maize and moved 40 soldiers into Guale villages to be fed. The Indigenous people complained bitterly to Rogel, who was forced to abandon his mission and move to Santa Elena rather than face rebellion. Menéndez, now strapped for cash, was unable to do any more for the colonists. All he could do to hold down costs was to limit the number of troops at each of the Florida forts.

Finally, in October 1570, Menéndez received a royal subsidy to support a full 150-man garrison at Santa Elena (Lyon 1984). Soldiers and supplies were sent to bring the fort back up to full strength, and Menéndez was able to arrange for more regular supply shipments from Havana.

Another Failed Attempt to Settle at Ajacán

In 1570, Menéndez summoned Don Luís, the captured Amerindian who had been living in Spain, to join a group of Jesuits under Father Juan Baptista de Segura, who planned to make another attempt at setting up a mission at Ajacán. The group included a small boy named Alonso de Olmos, the son of one of the settlers at Santa Elena, who had been trained by the fathers to serve at mass.

Upon their arrival, the missionaries were received warmly, and Don Luís proved very helpful. The missionaries with the Amerindians' help used lumber and nails brought from Cuba to build a house of at least two rooms and a chapel. Sadly, though, Don Luís soon bolted to reunite with his family and, in February 1571, led an ambush that killed the missionaries save for the altar boy (Wolfe 2021).

Menéndez Returns to Florida

Menéndez made his last visit to Florida in 1571. On May 7, he set sail from Spain with seven galleons, 250 sailors and soldiers, and 400 other settlers. He reached Havana on July 3, where he spent a few days getting another armada sent off, which was to escort the returning treasure fleet. During this time, he lost a few men by desertion and many others to illness. He also learned that the Guale had overwhelmed the Segura mission at Ajacán and killed the missionaries.

He first set sail for Santa Elena, which he reached on July 22.

> He found the small garrison at San Felipe in a satisfactory condition, and the natives humble and obedient, but engaged in war with the Indians friendly to the French ... who leave them to live in freedom, instead of my people and the Teatines (monks) ... who restrict their way of living [Lowery 1911, 272].

He then reinforced the garrison at San Felipe and headed to Ajacán to punish the locals for their massacre of the Dominicans. When he arrived, he found that the Amerindians had fled to the mountains. He disembarked with a company of soldiers to find them but was only able to capture eight. He did, however, rescue the child Alonso, who implicated the captives in the murders. Menéndez had them all hung from the yardarm of his ship after they had been converted and baptized.

In the late fall, Menéndez returned to St. Augustine and, after resupplying the garrison, set sail on December 20 for Havana with Alonso. While following the usual course to Cuba, his vessels were caught in a violent storm and were separated. One boat made it back to Havana, while one other wound up in the province of Ais, where the crew was attacked and killed.

The boat with Menéndez was cast ashore near Cape Canaveral, probably not far from where Ribault had shipwrecked. Menéndez and crew were able to land, build a makeshift fort with the wreckage, and, with a few undamaged arquebuses, defend themselves until nightfall when they set out towards St. Augustine, about 100 miles distant. Struggling onward through the wilderness they managed to reach St.

Augustine without the loss of a single life. In April 1572, a small rescue boat retrieved Menéndez and delivered him to Havana on Good Friday.

Menéndez then returned to Spain, where King Philip II appointed him captain-general of the armada that was to fight the Dutch, but on September 17, 1574, he died of typhoid before embarking.

The Changing of the Guard

When Menéndez died, his colony was left in far less able hands (Lyon 1988). Diego Velasco, his son-in-law, stepped in as interim lieutenant governor of Spanish Florida and briefly led a corrupt, duplicitous government. His administration ended in disgrace when Hernando de Miranda arrived to be permanent governor in 1576. Velasco and his treasurer, Bertolomeo Martinez, were imprisoned for corruption and crimes against the settlers and Indigenous people.

Soon war with the Guale and Orista-Escamazu people would eclipse all other concerns of Miranda. The fuse was lit when 21 men led by Sergeant Hernando Moyano helped themselves to corn gruel that the people of Escamazu had cooked for their evening meal (Lyon 1984). The Amerindians made no immediate response, but before dawn the next day, they slaughtered all the Spaniards except for one, who escaped and alerted the colony of the massacre. In a separate incident on Parris Island, an eight-man patrol with tracking dogs was ambushed and killed.

In the face of this growing danger, Miranda proved to be a weak leader and was frozen into inactivity—not able to execute any plan to save the colony. The day after the patrol was ambushed, all the people of Santa Elena deserted their homes and fled to Fort San Felipe. The Amerindians pillaged and set fire to the houses and then surrounded the fort. Miranda, breaking under the strain, could do nothing more than scream at the soldiers to defend the fort. Even though there were sufficient supplies and ammunition to withstand a siege of some days, everyone evacuated in small boats.

> As the Spaniards left in disorder, the Indians swarmed after them, firing arrows into the water. Then they set Fort San Felipe afire. As they sailed out of the sound, the last thing the surviving Spaniards saw was a smudge of smoke that marked the destruction of ten years of work and hope [Lyon 1984, 11].

The evacuees fled to St. Augustine, where Miranda took a ship for Spain. A few of the other settlers from Santa Elena remained in St. Augustine, but most of them fled to Cuba or Mexico.

Aftermath of the Siege on Santa Elena

One year after Santa Elena was destroyed, the king ordered it rebuilt, fearing that the French would fill the void and occupy the site. Philip II appointed Menéndez's nephew, Pedro Menéndez Márquez, governor of Florida. He had his soldiers build a new garrison, Fort San Marcos, and brought back more Spanish colonists to settle. Márquez, fearing attack by the locals, brought a prefabricated fort from St. Augustine and, with 53 men, erected it in just six days.

Mary Ross (1923, 256) describes the fort, renamed San Márquez:

> Near the blackened ruins of the old settlement, the Spanish standard was raised again, and floating high above the gleaming cannons of the new fortification, the proud banner of old Castile rose once more triumphant, all crimson and gold in the Carolina breeze, above the bristling ramparts of stern San Marcos.

Under the new governor's command, the Spanish soldiers began waging war against the local people, who were now harboring French castaways from the ship *Le Prince*, which had wrecked in Santa Elena harbor trying to return to Port Royal. Initially, the Orista and Guale had killed many of the survivors until they realized they were French, not Spanish. Those who were spared became valuable allies to the chiefdoms.

In 1579, Menéndez Márquez made several brutal expeditions against the Amerindians and French (Lyon 1988). He first ravaged the northern peninsula and Guale, seeking hidden Frenchmen, destroying food supplies and burning down 19 towns. He then attacked the villages of Oristan, defeating 300 bowmen with 65 soldiers. On August 26, he assaulted Cosaque, along the Coosawhatchie River northwest of Santa Elena, with 200 arquebusiers. Here, he sought 40 fugitive Frenchmen, burning down homes as he searched and killing any Frenchmen and locals he came upon. He was able to capture the French leader Captain Strozzi, who was taken back to St. Augustine for execution.

The governor then directed Captain Quirós, of the garrison at Santa Elena, to try to negotiate treaties with the Amerindians that included hostage-taking to ensure compliance (Lyon 1984). After another nasty assault upon Cosaque, its cacique begged for peace, offering seven captive Frenchmen and leaving behind his own son. Soon, caciques from Guale, Tolomato, and Tipique also agreed to treaties of peace.

La Florida into the 1580s

The combined French and Amerindian threats to Fort San Marquéz continued into the early 1580s, and military concerns became the focus of the second period of Santa Elena's Spanish occupation. The town had been rebuilt, and families had moved in, but they now lived completely under military rule. A period of guarded peace did not return to Santa Elena until early 1583, when Márquez launched another brutal war against the Orista and Guale chiefdoms, followed by a severe drought.

> It had taken fourteen years of colonization, but the Spaniards finally conquered the indigenous communities of the lower Carolina coast. Still, this was a hollow victory. Unlike Pedro Menéndez de Avilés, Marquês had no vision for Santa Elena, nor did the garrison serve any larger strategic or economic purpose. The coastal people, having failed either to incorporate Santa Elena into their world or to destroy it and expel the Spaniards, learned to live with them [Moore 2019, 21].

As the 1580s progressed, the English also began to seriously threaten the Spanish hold on southeastern America. Sir Walter Raleigh established his Roanoke colony in North Carolina in 1586, and from there, Sir Francis Drake began a war in the Caribbean. Drake started by attacking and pillaging Spanish settlements at Santo Domingo and Cartagena and then moved north. Fearing aggression in February 1586, Pedro Menéndez Márquez sent Miranda an urgent letter from St. Augustine to warn of an imminent attack (Lyon 1988). Miranda frantically worked for six weeks with a team of soldiers and Amerindians to strengthen and enlarge the fort at Santa Elena, building stockades, an earthen glacis, and raised cavaliers to fire out to sea.

In early June, Sir Francis Drake, with one thousand men, attacked and burned St. Augustine to the ground. He then headed north towards Santa Elena but overshot the harbor and was unable to return due to unfavorable winds (Lyon 1988). He proceeded on to Roanoke, where he picked up the desperate colonists and sailed back home (see next chapter).

TEN—Spanish Florida Staggers Toward the Seventeenth Century

Philip II ordered Santa Elena to be abandoned following Drake's raid. He felt that the two Florida garrisons should be joined into one at St. Augustine for better future defense. In August 1587, Pedro Menéndez Márquez destroyed the Spanish fort and town of Santa Elena and relocated its inhabitants to St. Augustine.

One must wonder what the fate of Santa Elena might have been if Pedro Menéndez had lived a few more years. As Lyon (1988, 16) eloquently put it:

> Perhaps the factor most lacking at Santa Elena after 1574 was that of the influence of Pedro Menéndez de Avilés.... Menéndez drew royal favor and private funds to the Florida enterprise. His vaulting ambition and the drive of his fervent obsession with Florida led to expansion beyond his means. Yet he did found Santa Elena, establish the colony there, and plan his own seat. Menéndez' immediate successors lacked his peculiar zeal and no longer held his privileges.

Spanish Mission System in Florida

As part of his strategy of conquest, Menéndez had hoped to establish a series of missions across southeastern North America, even before he had secured the frontiers. This goal would have a rocky path forward. It really wasn't until 1573, after Menéndez's death and the failed efforts of Jesuit Father Juan Rogel, that a band of Franciscan missionaries came to Santa Elena and achieved some success (Spellman 1965). In the beginning, their labors were confined to the coastal garrison towns of Santa Elena and St. Augustine. However, in 1595 the friars made a concerted effort to win over Florida's nations, and by the mid–seventeenth century, there were more than 30 missions serving 26,000 souls. The missions spread north of St. Augustine along the coast as far as St. Catherines Island, and across the interior to Apalachee Bay.

The Legacy of Pedro Menéndez de Avilés

There can be no doubt that Pedro Menéndez de Avilés's greatest achievement was as the architect of the great Armada de la Carrera, which carried the riches of Spanish America back to Spain. However, his attempt to settle La Florida and extract wealth from it was largely unfulfilled. He did successfully banish most of the French from La Florida and established a string of forts as far north as the island of St. Helena off present-day South Carolina; however, only St. Augustine persisted into the next century. In fact, St. Augustine was the only European settlement in North America in 1600 (Parker 2014).

Menéndez's settlements suffered from harassment from the local people, long and insufficient supply lines, and the lack of mineral riches. His attempts to convert the Indigenous people to Catholicism generally failed and he was not able to garner sufficient cooperation from the locals to generate any real wealth. While Spain grew rich from its mines in Mexico and South America, Florida generated little wealth.

As the seventeenth century progressed, Spain's control of Florida came to rely mainly on the mission system, which itself began to decline as the Indigenous population fell precipitously due to disease, poor management, and hurricane damage. There were several Spanish attempts to establish new settlements, but all failed. Having found no gold in the region, Spain increasingly came to view Florida and the presidio of St. Augustine not as a profit-generating possession but rather as a buffer between its much more prosperous colonies to the south and its rival French and English colonies to the north.

Eleven

The First English Intrusion into the Southeast
1584–1587

Setting the Stage

While Spain and France were sparring for control of southeastern Atlantic America throughout most of the sixteenth century, England was largely content to focus on its North Sea fisheries.

England did not emerge as a sea power until 1552, when Queen Elizabeth began sending the privateers John Hawkins and Francis Drake to seize and plunder Spanish and Portuguese ships off the coast of West Africa and then the Caribbean. As England began to flex its sea muscles, influential writers such as Richard Hakluyt (1552–1616) and John Dee (1527–1609) started pressuring Elizabeth to build her own overseas empire. To get into the action, Queen Elizabeth gave her blessing to three major expeditions within a decade of each other. Two of these were sent to the North Atlantic far from Spain's reach in La Florida— Martin Frobisher to Greenland and Baffin Island in 1576 and Humphrey Gilbert to Newfoundland in 1583. Only the third intruded directly into the territory claimed by Spain—the attempt of Sir Walter Raleigh to settle North Carolina in 1584.

Walter Raleigh was perhaps the most notable and colorful Elizabethan-era figure. Born in 1552, he came to serve the British royalty in multiple capacities, including fighting the rebellion in Ireland, defending England against the Spanish Armada, leading several missions as a privateer, and serving at the head of several efforts to colonize America. He became the most trusted adviser of Queen Elizabeth I and served in several political positions under her.

From Ponce de León to Sir Walter Raleigh

When his half-brother, Sir Humphrey Gilbert, was killed at sea after taking possession of Newfoundland in 1578 (Volume 2, Chapter 5), the way was cleared for Raleigh to seek his own grant to explore and settle America. He started his campaign by soliciting Hakluyt (the younger) to present to the queen a forceful argument for colonization of North America, titled *A Particuler Discourse Concerninge the Greate Necessitie and Manifolde Commodyties That Are Like to Growe to This Realme of Englande by the Westerne Discoueries Lately Attempted, Written in the Yere 1584.*

This document contained 21 points, making the case for the colonization of North America. Among the most important were:

- Colonization could enlarge the reach of the reformed church, of which Queen Elizabeth was the principal.
- North America had all the commodities that England needed.
- The colonies could employ many currently idle men.
- If England had its own New World ports, Spanish ships coming from the Caribbean could be more easily intercepted.
- England could find its own source of gold, ending Spanish dominance.
- Spanish control of the West Indies could be more effectively disrupted.
- England could easily expand north of 23 degrees, where there were no Spanish settlements.
- Spanish cruelties in the West Indies were worse than those of the Turks in the Holy Land.
- Ireland would be a perfect jumping-off point for sailing west, without interfering with other nations' trade.
- The queen could increase customs revenue from New World trade.
- England could find a Northwest Passage to China.
- If England gained land in the Western Hemisphere, it would force Spain to give up on the old papal bull that gave the West Indies to the kings of Spain.

Raleigh's campaign was successful, and by December [he] had the support of both the Crown and the House of Commons, and on January 6, 1585, he was knighted during a celebration of the Twelfth Night of Christmas; shortly afterward, he assumed the title, Lord and Governor of Virginia, that revealed a new name for the queen's colony [Wolfe 2022].

Eleven—The First English Intrusion into the Southeast

Queen Elizabeth granted him a royal charter like she had previously given Gilbert (Volume 2, Chapter 5), authorizing him to explore, colonize, and rule any "remote, heathen and barbarous lands, countries and territories, not actually possessed of any Christian Prince or inhabited by Christian People, in return for one-fifth of all the gold and silver that might be mined there" ("Charter to Sir Walter Raleigh: 1584" 2022). This charter stipulated that Raleigh had seven years in which to establish a settlement or else lose his right to do so.

The grant to Raleigh was part of a three-pronged strategy of Elizabeth in her war against Spain. The queen planned to send an army to the Netherlands to fight for the Protestants; Sir Francis Drake and other privateers would be sent to the West Indies to attack Spanish shipping; and colonists would be sent to the Chesapeake region to harvest local riches and establish a safe harbor for the English privateers. She also hoped the colonists would discover gold and silver and convert as many local people as possible to the Christian religion ("Charter to Sir Walter Raleigh: 1584" 2022).

The First English Expedition to Southern Atlantic America

Elizabeth directed Sir Walter in 1584 to organize the first English expedition to North America. He put captains Philip Amadas and Arthur Barlowe in charge of two ships and sent them off on April 21 (Evans 2006). Also on board were the noted English mathematician, astronomer, and linguist Thomas Harriot and the artist and mapmaker John White.

Several extraordinary eyewitness reports would be published of this first English expedition to North America. Thomas Harriot produced *A Briefe and True Report of the New Found Land of Virginia*, published in 1588, and Arthur Barlowe wrote *The First Voyage Made to the Coastes of America*, which appeared a year later. John White executed many paintings and sketches of the lands, Indigenous peoples, flora, and fauna of the region. These were reproduced as etchings in 1590 by Theodor de Bry in a reprint of Harriot's *A Briefe and True Report*.

Amadas and Barlowe took the southern route to North America, passing through the Canaries and West Indies before landing on July 4, 1584, on the Outer Banks of present-day North Carolina. They likely

From Ponce de León to Sir Walter Raleigh

first visited Wococon Island (Ocracoke), about 60 miles south of Roanoke Island. They found the shore of Wococon to be sandy and flat, but the "Island had many goodly woods full of deer, conies, hares, and fowle, even in the middle of summer in incredible abundance" (Barlowe 1880, 3). After enjoying the sight, they fired a musket shot at a flock of cranes, producing "such a cry redoubled by many echoes, as if an army of men had shouted all together."

On July 7, 1584, they saw their first Amerindians:

> We spied one small boat rowing towards us, having in it three persons: this boat came to the land's side, four harquebuses shot from our ships, and they're two of the people remaining, the third came along the shore side towards us, and we being then all within the board, he walked up and down upon the point of the land next unto us: then the Master, and the Pilot of

The arrival of the English at Roanoke in 1590. John White's map shows Virginia's coast with many islands just off the mainland, two native territories (Secotan and Weapemeoc), and the native community of Roanoke on an island at the mouth of a river; Theodor de Bry, *Wunderbarliche, doch warhafftige Erklärung, von der Gelegenheit und Sitten der Wilden in Virginia ... / Erstlich in engelländischer Sprach beschrieben durch Thomam Hariot, und newlich durch Christ*, 1590, [plate] 2) (Wikimedia Commons).

the Admiral, Simon Fernández, and the Captain Philip Amadas, myself, and others rowed to the land, whose coming this fellow attended, never making any show of fear or doubt. And after he had spoken of many things not understood by us, we brought him, with his own good liking, aboard the ships, and gave him a shirt, a hat, and some other things, and made him a taste of our wine, and our meat, which he liked very well: and after having viewed both barks, he departed and went to his own boat again, which he had left in a little Cove, or Creek adjoining: as soon as he was two bows shot into the water, he fell to fishing, and in less than half an hour, he had laden his boat as deep, as it could swim, with which he came again to the point of the land, and there he divided his fish into two parts, pointing one part to the ship, and the other to the Pinnace: which after he had (as much as he might,) requited the former benefits received, he departed out of our sight [Barlowe 1880, 3].

First Visit by Granganimeo

The next day, the English were visited by Granganimeo, the brother of Wingina, the chief of the local Roanoke. Wingina was head of villages at Secotan and Dasemunkepeuc on the mainland and another village on the north end of Roanoke Island, Ossomocomuck. He was accompanied by 40 to 50 men whom Barlowe (1880, 4) described as handsome and fine-looking:

When he came to the place, his servants spread a long matte upon the ground, on which he sat down, and at the other end of the mat, four others of his company did the like: the rest of his men stood round about him, somewhat far off: when we came to the shore to him with our weapons, he never moored from his place, nor any of the other four, nor never mistrusted any harm to be offered from us, but sitting still he beckoned us to come, and sit by him, which we performed: and being settled, he makes all signs of joy, and welcome, striking on his head and his breast and afterward on ours, to showed we were all one, smiling, and making shows the best he could of all love, and familiarity.

A few days later, Granganimeo came aboard the English ship, bringing with him his wife and children:

After two or three days, the King's brother came aboard our ships, and drank wine, and eat of our meat and of our bread, and liked exceedingly thereof: and after a day passed, he brought his wife with him to the ships, his daughter, and two or three little children: his wife was very favored, of mean stature, and very bashful: she had on her back a long cloak of leather, with the fur side next to her body, and before her, a piece of the same: about her forehead she had a broad band of white coral, and so had her husband many times: in her ears she had bracelets of pearls, hanging down to her middle.... The rest of her women of the better sort, had pendants of copper, hanging in every ear, and some of the children of the King's brother, and other noblemen, have five or six in every ear: he himself had upon his head, a broad plate of gold, or copper, for being unpolished, we knew not what metal it should be, nor would he by any means suffer us to take it off his head, but feeling it, it would bow very easily. His apparel was as his wives, only the women wear their hair long on both sides, and the men but on one. They are of color yellowish, and their hair black for the most, and yet we saw children that have very fine auburn and chestnut color hair [Barlowe 1880, 5].

On July 13, 1584, the explorers followed an inlet leading to the island called Roanoke by the locals. Barlowe and seven of his companions sailed towards the northern end of the island, where they found the Amerindian village of Ossomocomuck surrounded by a palisade:

And the evening following we came to an Island which they call Roanoak, distant from the harbor by which we entered, seven leagues: and at the North end thereof was a village of nine houses, built of Cedar, and fortified roundabout with sharp trees, to keep out their enemies, and the entrance into it made like a turnpike very artificially; when we came towards it, standing near unto the side of the water, the wife of Granganimo the Kings brother came running out to meet us very cheerfully and friendly, her husband was not then in the village; some of her people she commanded to draw our boat on shore for the beating of the billow: others she appointed to carry us on their backs to the dry ground, and others to bring our oars into the house for fear of stealing. When we were come into the other room, having five rooms in her house, she caused us to sit down by a great fire, and after took off our clothes and washed them, and dried them again: some of the women plucked off our stockings and washed them, some washed our feet in warm water, and she herself took great pains to see all things ordered in the best manner she could, making great haste to dress some meat for us to eat [Barlowe 1880, 7].

All in all, the visit to the North Bank must have left Amadas and Barlowe with a strong sense that the Indigenous people would be friendly and helpful in any subsequent settlement attempts. The principal chief of the Roanoke, Wingina, had decided that the English were not a threat to him and, in fact, could become important trading partners and perhaps valuable allies.

In mid–August 1584, Amadas and Barlowe returned to England,

with two local Amerindians onboard, Manteo and Wanchese. Wanchese was of the Roanoke people and perhaps a werowance, while Manteo was from Croatoan, a smaller, related nation. They had been sent by Wingina, and "their assignment was to cross over into English culture and bring back as much intelligence as possible about these strangers who might become useful allies" (Lowery 2018, 23). Because the English explorers had treated the Amerindians of the Roanoke region with respect and dignity, Wingina likely saw promise in the English as allies in war.

> These new strangers did not appear to be a threat but simply seemed scared and weak. Further, Barlowe had arrived at an opportune time. Wingina had been engaged in a bitter and deadly war with the Pomeioocs, who lived on the Neuse River. A few years earlier, the Pomeioocs and their allies escalated the war by killing thirty Secotan warriors at a peace conference [Lowery 2018, 23].

Wingina was allied with the Secotan.

Upon arriving in London, Manteo and Wanchese became guests of Sir Walter at his home, Durham House, where he kept them under rigid control and made them dress as Englishmen. He intended to use them as a hook to drum up financial support for his colonial adventures and as a soundboard to learn as much as possible about the culture of the Indigenous people of southern Virginia. Sir Walter enlisted Thomas Harriot to learn the Algonquian language from the two and compose a dictionary. Harriot sat long hours daily with them to learn as much as possible about the Roanoke Island region and the people who lived there.

Sir Walter's Second Expedition to Virginia

In his second expedition, Sir Walter was intent on colonization, not just exploration. He wanted to establish and fortify a site on the fringe of Spanish Florida that would prevent the Spanish from gaining any ground there. "He thought he had secured Wingina's friendship and Manteo's and Wanchese's loyalty. He did not think to ask their permission" (Lowery 2018, 24).

On April 9, 1585, 600 colonists sailed from Plymouth with Manteo and Wanchese in seven ships. About half the colonists were soldiers, but all the trades were represented, including "carpenters, smiths, cooks, shoemakers, and at least one minister" (Wolfe 2022). Sir Richard Grenville, Raleigh's cousin, commanded the flagship *Tyger*, piloted by Simão Fernandes; the 100-ton *Lyon* was commanded and owned by George Raymond; the 50-ton *Elizabeth* was commanded and outfitted by Thomas Cavendish, who would later circumnavigate the globe in 1586–88 CE; the 140-ton *Roebuck* was commanded by John Clark; and the 50-ton *Dorothy* and two smaller pinnaces were owned by Raleigh himself.

Colonel Ralph Lane, recently the sheriff of County Kerry, Ireland, was made second-in-command of the mission. Also aboard was John White, the celebrated cartographer and artist who had accompanied Martin Frobisher in his search for the Northwest Passage in the 1570s, and Thomas Harriot, who had debriefed Mateo and Wanchese and was the only Englishman who knew Algonguian.

Harriot wrote a report on the mission named *A Briefe and True Report of the New Found Land of Virginia*, which was published in 1590. *True Report* contained an early account of the extractable resources of the area and the local people, whom Harriot assessed thus: "If means of good government be used, … they may in a short time be brought to civility and the embracing of true religion" (Harriot 1590, 25).

The ships sailed south to the Canary Islands and from there westward to the West Indies. Along the way, a violent storm separated the fleet, and one of the pinnaces was swamped and sank. Grenville in the *Tyger* sailed alone to the proposed rendezvous point at Spanish-held Puerto Rico. He built a temporary fort there, constructed a new pinnace, and plundered a few Spanish vessels and ports. About a week after its arrival, *Elizabeth* joined the *Tyger*, having been separated a month earlier.

Grenville spent over a month in the Caribbean, and "alarm bells began to go off in the minds of Spanish officials in the area":

> What were the English up to? Rumor had it that the English were going to establish a settlement on the East Coast of North America, so why were they spending so much time in the West Indies? Were they also planning an attack on Spanish possessions in the area? Warnings to be on the alert for an English attack were issued to all governors. Pedro Menéndez Marqués, the governor of the Spanish settlement at St. Augustine, began to gather men and supplies for an expedition to discover any settlement the English might have established on the east coast and destroy it [Pickett and Pickett 2011, 104].

ELEVEN—The First English Intrusion into the Southeast

Grenville made no attacks on any Spanish fortifications, but in 1586, Sir Francis Drake raided Cartagena in present-day Colombia and St. Augustine in Florida.

In mid–July, the English finally made their way to the Outer Banks of North Carolina. There, in the treacherous shallows, Fernandes ran the *Tyger* aground, and most of the colonists' foodstuffs were lost when seawater seeped into the ship's stores. The colonists now had only enough food for just 20 days rather than the original full year. As the *Tyger* was being repaired, they learned that Captain Raymond of the *Lyon* had dropped off about 30 colonists on Croatoan Island on his way to plunder Spanish ships.

The English reappeared in North Carolina, with the local people now feeling ambivalent about their presence. Wingina had held firm in his desire to work with the English, but the other Algonquian leaders were much more combative. Their anxiety had received strong celestial support in an eclipse while the English were gone and the arrival of a comet when the English reappeared. A mysterious quick-killing disease, which was probably introduced during the first English appearance, had also begun ravaging the villages (Wolfe 2022).

On July 11, Sir Richard led a mission to Pamlico Sound to find a good site for colonization. This is the same sound that Verrazzano thought was the entry to the Pacific Ocean in 1524 (Morison 1971). They traveled about 25 miles north and landed 60 men, including Manteo. They discovered the Amerindian village of Ossomocomuck near Lake Mattamuskeet, home of Wingina's rival Piemacum, and then the village of Aquascogoc. The group then continued on to the Pungo River, one of the branches of the Pamlico River, and discovered another village named Secotan.

Here, Grenville "committed an act of ruthless folly which began the ruin of friendly relations with the natives so carefully built up by Amadas and Barlowe" (Morison 1971, 642). A silver cup disappeared from one of the boats, and when the local werowance did not immediately return it, Grenville burned down their village and destroyed their corn. Even though the colony would be dependent on future Amerindian cooperation, Grenville chose to teach them a lesson rather than be patient and benevolent.

Such arrogant, unconscionable actions would be committed repeatedly by English settlers over the colonial period.

Bounteous initial hospitality always seemed to convince Europeans that they could be freeloaders indefinitely, that as superior beings, they should be provided with fish, corn, venison, or whatever they wanted. But though they paid with knives, bells, and beads, consumer demand was soon satisfied [Morison 1971, 647].

Despite Grenville's grievous act, on July 21, he and Manteo met with Granganimeo, who permitted them to occupy the north end of Roanoke, about half a mile from Wingina's town. Grenville then returned to England for more supplies, leaving Ralph Lane in charge of 108 men and a pinnace to further explore the region. On his way home, Grenville captured the Spanish ship *Santa Maria de San Vicente*, which proved to be a great prize, yielding some £50,000. This ship's capture underlined Sir Walter's belief from the beginning that colonization and exploration could be financed through privateering.

Details of what happened after Grenville's departure from Roanoke are sketchy, with conflicting scenarios often presented (Morison 1971; Lowery 2018; Wolfe 2022). It is known that the colonists were surprised at the mildness of the winter, and they may have successfully planted some corn and ratoons of banana they had obtained in Puerto Rico. They also built a fort on the northern end of Roanoke Island. Manteo fulfilled Raleigh's hopes by helping the colonists establish friendly relations with the local people and begin trade. Wanchese apparently chose to rejoin his people.

Manteo served as an interpreter for the colonial leaders as they began exploring the Virginia coast and played an integral role in their safety during their stay in Roanoke. Manteo also made an important impact by assisting John White in painting the flora, fauna, and the Algonquian people. White made 75 drawings that represent the most accurate depictions of early America's Indigenous people, "capturing their dress, towns, fishing techniques, agriculture, ritual dances, and ceremonial figures, unlike anything possible without the knowledge and access provided by someone like Manteo" (Wolfe 2022).

Exploration into Albemarle Sound

That winter, Amadas led a mission through Albemarle Sound, and down the Chowan River into the land of Menatonon, the werowance of Chowanoc, the largest village along the river. When Lane arrived, he found a large gathering of Menatonon's Mangoak, along with several other groups, including the Montauk from the south and some Weapemeoc from the west.

It is not known why this group had assembled, but the audacious Lane immediately "stormed into the center of the gathering and took the elderly Menatonon as his prisoner" (Oberg 2007, 81). Once in custody, Menatonon told Lane what he wanted to hear and convinced him that he was a friend and that Wingina was actually the enemy. He pointed out that he could have easily prevented the Englishmen from entering his village and could have massacred their small group if he had wanted. He also regaled Lane with a story that copper could be easily mined along the nearby River of Morattico.

Lane decided to search for the copper mines and took Menatonon's son Skiko hostage to ensure his soldiers wouldn't fall victim to some sort of treachery. He carried little food but unrealistically expected the Amerindians to come to his aid as he ascended the river. They, of course, offered no such aid and, two days into the trip, assaulted Lane's group with a volley of arrows launched from the cover of the forested shore. The arrows did little damage to the party, but the attack convinced Lane that it was time to return to Roanoke.

Affairs at Roanoke

While Lane was gone, disease and famine had continued to take a heavy toll on the Roanoke. Granganimeo died early in 1586, and Wingina, who now called himself Pemisapan, began thinking seriously about wiping out the intruders. He came to believe that the English were responsible for the epidemic since they remained healthy and that it was within their power to mitigate the plague. While Manteo continued to do his best to maintain friendly relations, Pemisapan chose to stop giving the colonists food, greatly raising their anxiety levels as they struggled to feed themselves.

Lane became convinced that Pemisapan was either plotting to attack his weak colony or betray it to Amerindians further west. He rebuffed a group of emissaries sent by Menatonon to ransom Skiko and then sent 25 men, with Manteo as a guide, to assault Pemisapan's village of Dasemunkepeuc. In the ensuing onslaught, Pemisapan was chased down and beheaded by an Irish colonist named Edward Nugent, who impaled the head on a spike.

As the settlers fearfully waited for the repercussions of their attack, Sir Francis Drake miraculously appeared at Roanoke in June of 1586, fresh from raids against the Spanish at Cartagena on the coast of today's Colombia and St. Augustine in Florida. To the colonists' great relief, he offered them passage to England. They jumped at the chance, hungry and fearing retribution from the locals. Manteo went with them, returning to England for a second time. Skiko was likely hanged before the ships embarked, after trying to break for his freedom.

To make room for the colonists in his ships, Drake may, David Quinn (1974) suggested, have left behind on the Outer Banks several hundred African slaves and Amerindians captured at Cartagena. Other historians contend that these people either drowned in a storm or were sold on the way to England (Lawler 2018). Oberg (2007, 102) called these people "the first and almost entirely forgotten Lost Colony." It is remarkable that there is so little record of their existence.

Only a few weeks after Lane and the original colonists had fled, Grenville arrived back at Roanoke with 200 more colonists and provisions. He hung around for a few weeks, dithering about what to do, but ultimately decided to take most of the colonists back to England. He left behind a garrison of just 15 men and enough supplies to keep the colony going for supposedly two years. It will be no surprise that these men were never heard from again. It is likely that they were attacked and killed by a vengeful group of Amerindians, perhaps led by Wanchese, who needed to prove his loyalty to his kin. When he dropped the men off, Grenville would not have known of Lane's ambush of Pemisapan and his people.

Sir Walter's Third Expedition—The Lost Colony

Sir Walter Raleigh must have been furious when Lane and the original Roanoke colonists returned to England, followed by Grenville and what were supposed to be reinforcements. Had they all not fled, there would have been more than 300 colonists at Roanoke with supplies to last a year or more. A huge investment had been frittered away. Still, there was the massive wealth contained in Drake's South American booty to keep the Crown happy.

"Despite the trials and tribulations of the first attempt at a settlement, interest was piqued by the returning colonists who showed off

ELEVEN—The First English Intrusion into the Southeast

such novelties as tobacco and potatoes" (Cartwright 2020). New prospective colonists were ready to start anew, so Raleigh masterminded another expedition in 1587 with the aid of trusty Manteo, now accustomed to the English language and culture. One has to be astonished that this new settlement was planned so quickly, with so little concern about the Amerindians on the Outer Banks and their growing disenchantment with the English invasion.

John White was to be the colony's governor, presiding over 117 settlers, this time composed of both men and women—89 men, 17 women, and 11 children. Each male would receive at least 500 acres of land, with the rights of the Indigenous people not at all considered. The plan was to establish the city of Raleigh on the Chesapeake Bay, where the Amerindians might be friendlier and the water more suitable for deep water navigation.

The expedition first returned to Roanoke to check on Grenville's men but found no signs of them. It was then decided by Captain Fernandes of the *Lyon* that the colonists would remain at Roanoke. Historians have debated the reason for this decision, but probably by this point, the summer was almost over, and Fernandes was probably anxious to get back to the West Indies to loot Spanish ships.

The colonists and Manteo were deposited back on Roanoke Island on July 22, 1587. Of course, the Roanoke could not have forgotten Lane's raid on their village and the murder of their people back in 1585, so it is hard to believe that the colonists really expected to establish peaceful trading partnerships. As a harbinger of what was to come, White's adviser George Howe was found on July 28 in the woods near camp, dead from 16 arrows and a gruesome beating.

To find out who was responsible, White sailed south three days later to meet with the Chroatoans, who reported that both Grenville's men and Howe had been killed by Roanokes at Dasemunkepeuc. They promised to support the English on one condition: "that there might be some token or badge is given them of us, whereby we might know them to be our friends when we met them anywhere out of the Town or Island." White responded by "saying that English fury fell only on those who offended them and that English friends need not worry" (Lowery 2018, 25).

White then decided it was time to retaliate for the murder of the English soldiers left behind by Lane. In the dead of night on August 9, Manteo led White and some of his men across the water to

Dasemunkepeuc, where they attacked the town. To their horror, they discovered too late that the village was now occupied by friendly Croatoans and not enemy Roanoke. The Roanoke had deserted the village just before the attack, and Croatoans had replaced them in search of maize (Pickett and Pickett 2011). Although this turn of events deeply grieved Manteo, he stayed with the English, and on August 13 he was baptized into the Church of England and named lord of Roanoke and Dasemunkepeuc (Lowery 2018).

> Five days after Manteo's baptism, John White's daughter, Eleanor Dare, gave birth to a girl, and he named her Virginia. Her parents could hardly have imagined worse circumstances for their little girl. Under the haze of cultural superiority, the leaders of this expedition alienated the only people who could help the settlers survive.
> Certain that they could no longer expect any help from the local people, the settlers demanded that White return to England for more supplies and he agreed. [Lowery 2018, 25–26].

Upon his return to England, White searched frantically for a relief ship, but because of England's war with Spain, there were no ships to spare. Three years passed before he could find one, and when he finally got back to Roanoke in 1590, he could find no surviving settlers. All the colonists were gone, giving Roanoke the epithet of "the lost colony." The only trace of their fate was a mysterious "cro" carved in a tree, and "croatoan" carved in a fence post.

As described by John White in his journal of the voyage:

> From hence we went through the woods to that part of the Land directly over against Dasamongwepeuk, and from thence we returned by the waterside, round about the northpoint of the land until we came to the place where I left our Colony in the year 1586 ... and as we entered up the sandy bank upon a tree, in the very brow thereof were curiously carved these faire Roman letters CRO: which letters presently we knew to signify the place, where I should find the planters seated ... we passed toward the place where they were left in sundry houses, but we found the houses taken down and the place very strongly enclosed with a high palisade of great trees, with cortices and flankers very fort-like, and one of the chief trees or posts at the right side of the entrance had the bark taken off, and 5 foot from the ground in capital letters was graven CROATOAN without any crosse or sign of distress ... We went along ... to see if we could find any of their boats or Pinnaces, but we could perceive no sign of them, nor any of the small Ordinance which were left with them.... At our return from the creek, some of our sailors meeting us, told that they had found where divers chests had been hidden, and long since dug up again and broken up, and much of the

goods in them spoiled and scattered about, but nothing left, of such things as the Savages knew any use of, undefaced ... this could be no other but the deed of the Savages our enemies at Dasamongwepeuk, who had watched the departure of our men to Croatoan; and as soon as they were departed, dug up every place where they suspected anything to be buried [Burrage 1906, 317].

White desperately wanted to believe that the colonists had migrated southward to Croatoan Island, led by their Indian associate, Manteo. He sailed in the direction of the island, but bad weather and the growing anxiety of the sailors prevented him from searching it. With the hurricane season approaching, he felt he had no choice but to depart for England.

Looking back, it seems possible that at least some of the lost colony members could have gone south to live on the Outer Banks and intermarry with the native people. However, it is just as likely that they were murdered or enslaved. Nobody has ever definitely discovered the final fate of the Roanoke colonists, although recent research has uncovered some of their belongings in the remains of Croatoan villages (Jarus 2021). This suggests either that they moved and became assimilated with the local people, or they were simply murdered and their belongings snatched. A massacre would seem appropriate considering the previous conduct of the English towards the local people.

Later Searches for the Roanoke Settlers

From the Jamestown colony that was established 20 years later, several expeditions were sent out to search for the Roanoke colonists, and all came up empty-handed. However, Samuel Purchas reported in his *Pilgrimes* or *Hakluytus Posthumus* (1624), based on John Smith's written notes, that "Powhatan confessed that he had been at the murder of that Colony and showed to Captain Smith a musket barrel and brass mortar and certain pieces of iron which had been theirs" (McCartney 2005).

Lifeways of the Roanoke and Croatoans

The Roanoke were a Carolina Algonquian-speaking people who lived in present-day Dare County, Roanoke Island, and part of the mainland at the time of English exploration (Evans 2006). They were one of many Algonquian nations in eastern North Carolina, which numbered 5,000 to 10,000 people. A small, related group, the Croatoans also lived in the coastal areas of what is now North Carolina. They probably inhabited present-day Hatteras and Ocracoke Islands at the time of the English arrival.

The region was dotted with numerous autonomous villages of all sizes, most of them small and temporary, but largely self-sufficient. Each nation was led by a leader or commander called a werowance, who ruled a varying number of villages.

As described by Harriot, with modernized spelling (1590, 24):

> Their towns are but small, and near the seacoast but few, some containing but 10 or 12 houses: some 20, the greatest that we have seen have been but 30 houses.... Their houses are made of small poles made fast at the tops in round form after the manner as is used in many arbors in our gardens of England, in most towns covered with bark, and in some with artificial mattes made of long rushes; from the tops of the houses down to the ground. The length of them is commonly double the breadth, in some places they are but 12 and 16 yards long, and in others some we have seen of four and twenty.
>
> In some places of the country, one only town belonged to the government of a weroance or chief Lord; in others some two or three, in some six, eight, & more; the greatest weroance that yet we had dealing with had but eighteen towns in his government, and able to make not about seven or eight hundred fighting men at the most: The language of every government is different from any other, and the farther they are distant the greater is the difference.

John White made detailed drawings of two very different Indian towns—Pomeiooc, which was surrounded by a palisade of stripped, sharpened logs, and Secotan, which did not have a stockade but covered a much greater area. Pomeiooc consisted of 18 buildings arranged around a circular clearing. Outside of its wall were agricultural fields and an artificial water hole. Secotan consisted of a main street surrounded by cornfields, plots of tobacco and squash, and scattered houses. A boy is depicted in a hut to ward off birds and other animals. The houses in both villages were similar to those of the Powhatan in Virginia, a bark or a matt-covered framework of poles that were bent over and lashed together.

The Roanoke had a yearly round of subsistence activities (Oberg 2007). In the late winter and early spring, they lived primarily on fish,

ELEVEN—The First English Intrusion into the Southeast

particularly on sturgeon and herring. They used weirs to trap fish but also speared them from their dugout canoes. They also hunted turkeys, squirrels, and rabbits and harvested crabs and shellfish, which were abundant. They planted their fields in May and June, subsisting during these months on acorns, walnuts, berries, fish, and any maize they still had in storage. After clearing the fields, like the Powhatan, they put four corn seeds in holes made with sticks about a yard apart and planted squash, beans, and sunflower around them. Considerable effort was taken by women to keep the fields weed-free. While the women and children tended the fields, the men went off to hunt deer, rabbits, black bears, and waterfowl. The women also made mats, baskets, pots, and mortars; they also harvested the crops and prepared meals.

Epilogue
Southern Atlantic America in the Seventeenth Century

Setting the Stage: Events in the Sixteenth Century

Florida was first reached by the Spaniard Ponce de León in 1512 following the route pioneered by slavers searching the Florida Strait for a new source of captives. Ponce was looking for mineral wealth, but vigorous attacks by the Indigenous Calusa and Ais prevented him from establishing a base of operations.

Following Ponce to North America was slave trader Pedro de Salazar, who stumbled onto what became called the "Land of Chicora" along the border of Georgia and South Carolina. He returned with reports of docile and friendly Indigenous people who lived in a verdant, rich landscape. Excited by these reports, Lucas Vázquez de Ayllón sent several missions to further explore the region and then led another expedition himself to colonize. He was able to establish the first North American colony at Sapelo Sound in Georgia; however, it survived for less than three months, plagued by food shortages, unhealthy living conditions, physical exhaustion, and ambush.

In 1524, Italian Giovanni da Verrazzano, sailing for France, was the first to hop-skip up the entire Eastern Seaboard from Atlantic America from the Outer Banks of North Carolina to Cape Cod, then New York Harbor and the Gulf of Maine. This incredible voyage made it abundantly clear that there was a major continent between Europe and the Far East.

Ponce de León was then followed into Florida by Hernando de Soto, Pánfilo de Narváez, Tristán de Luna, and Pedro Menéndez. All were part of a Spanish push to explore and settle southeastern America and protect

Epilogue

the shipping lanes of their treasure fleet. De Soto made a massive drive into the American Southeast in search of gold but came up empty-handed after brutalizing the great agricultural societies he met along the way. Pánfilo de Narváez would lead a mission in 1527 that was a total fiasco. His expedition started with about 600 men and ended eight years later with only chronicler Cabeza de Vaca and three others alive. The survivors endured an arduous journey by rafts across the Gulf of Mexico and then a long, naked trek across the American Southwest to Mexico City.

Luna was charged with landing 1,500 colonists at Ochuse in Pensacola Bay, traveling to Coosa in northern Alabama, and then forging a route to Punta de Santa Elena in South Carolina. On paper, it seemed like a good way for Spain to solidify its ownership of La Florida, but it turned into a nightmare when Luna tried to carry it out. Disaster struck early when a hurricane destroyed half of their supplies. The distances between Ochuse, Coosa, and the Punta de Santa Elena proved to be much greater than the Spaniards realized, and the native people were fewer in number and less manageable than they expected.

In 1562, the admiral of France, Gaspard Coligny de Châtillon, a leader of the early French Protestant (Huguenot) movement, commissioned Jean Ribault and later René Goulaine de Laudonnière to challenge the Spanish colonial claims on Florida by establishing colonies there. What unfolded was a long saga of disappointment, bloodshed, and failure as the French tried to manipulate the local Guale and Timucua. Ultimately, their first colony at Charlesfort failed when the starving colonists fled. A second attempt at colonization at Parris Island was teetering on the brink of starvation when Pedro Menéndez de Avilés and the Spanish arrived and destroyed it.

Spanish King Philip II sent Pedro Menéndez de Avilés and one thousand soldiers and settlers to uphold Spain's long-standing claim to Florida. Menéndez destroyed the French colony, massacring most of its occupants, and then established a network of new colonies along the eastern coast of Florida. He tried hard to maintain good working relationships with the Indigenous people, even marrying the sister of the Calusa's paramount chief, Carlos. He put considerable effort into making Santa Elena the capital of La Florida and keeping St. Augustine strong as a presidio. However, he struggled mightily to keep his colonies afloat, as they were all chronically undersupplied and continuously hassled by the surrounding Amerindians. His "Enterprise of Florida" staggered under frequent bouts of desertions, mutinies, and ambushes by the local people. Only his first settlement of St. Augustine would ultimately endure.

English into the South

As the sixteenth century progressed, the English became convinced that the climate of the mid–Atlantic would prove to be more favorable for colonization than that of the cold North. In 1584, Queen Elizabeth directed Sir Walter Raleigh to send the first English expedition to the mid–Atlantic. This group landed on the Outer Banks of North Carolina and had very friendly interactions with the local Roanoke people. Encouraged by this welcome, Sir Walter dispatched another group of colonists the following year. Things appeared to start out well for this group, but when a supply ship returned to the colony after five years away, it was found to be abandoned. No one knows for sure what happened to these colonists, but the most likely explanation is that relations with the Roanoke became contentious, and all the settlers were massacred.

The Central Role of South Carolina

It is largely unrecognized that South Carolina was a focus of both the Spanish and French in the early period of North American conquest. What was initially called the Land of Chicora was first visited by Pedro de Salazar in 1521, only a decade after Ponce's discovery of La Florida. His discovery led to the first Spanish settlement in North America, San Miguel de Gualdape, established at Sapelo Sound on the Georgia coast by Lucas Vázquez de Ayllón. The colony only lasted a few months, but the Spanish did not long forget its strategic importance on the east coast of America. One of the unfulfilled intentions of the Luna expedition was to reestablish a colony in the area referred to as Punta Santa Elena. In 1562, the Frenchman René Goulaine de Laudonnière stunned the Spanish when he established a colony on Parris Island, South Carolina, but it was soon destroyed by Spaniard Pedro Menéndez and rebuilt as Fort Santa Elena. He subsequently populated it with a thousand settlers, and it would serve as the northernmost Spanish colony in the Americas until it was abandoned in 1587.

Epilogue

La Florida into the Seventeenth Century

As the sixteenth century ended, St. Augustine was the only settlement remaining in La Florida and, in fact, across the rest of Atlantic America. English Jamestown and French Québec would not be established until 1607 and 1608, respectively. Over the next century, St. Augustine would have to endure a government inquiry into whether it was worth supporting at all, being burned to the ground by English privateers, multiple assaults from Amerindians, and a number of epidemics.

At the ripe old age of 35 in 1600, St. Augustine had endured far longer than any other European settlement.

However, when La Florida's new governor, Gonzalo Méndez de Canço arrived in 1597, the city was in a pitiful state. Recruiting people to go to the Spanish frontier was almost impossible; New Spain and Peru, with their documented wealth, were much more popular. Only through royal support could the city endure as a military post (presidio). The king could not afford to leave La Florida unprotected and subject to English or French occupation. The peninsula was located along the route that the Spanish fleets used to carry the bounty of the Indies to Spain. The establishment of the English in Virginia in 1607 "ensured Spain's continued financial and material support for La Florida" (Parker 2014, 560).

Conditions at St. Augustine

Pickett and Pickett (2011, 93) describe the situation in St. Augustine in the late sixteenth century as deplorable:

> Soldiers and settlers both wanted to mutiny, but there was nowhere for them to go on land, and the officials were careful to see that there were no ships to steal. The only way to leave was to pay a ransom to the governor. Lucky was the soldier or settler who had enough money from what he brought with him from Spain and was able to collect it together with his pay and give it to the governor in return for permission to leave.
>
> The fort was surrounded by water on three sides and prone to flooding. The land was wooded and low, filled with roots, and could only be cultivated on a sandy part owned mostly by the governor, who had soldiers cultivate it for him. The settlers were given garden plots but, at most, could grow some pumpkins and perhaps 20 pounds of corn. Most vegetables did

not do well. They spent most of their time grinding corn and catching fish for protein.

There were about 50 cows grazing on one of the islands, but they were not for the use of the soldiers and settlers, being killed only when the governor wished it. The cows were thin and undernourished and rarely gave birth; those calves that were born generally died from lack of food. There was no fresh water on the island, so the herd was only able to get water when it rained. In 1572, it was reported that there were 50 pigs, but they were only slaughtered for the governors' table and suffered from lack of food and water and attacks from predators.... The soldiers and settlers worked hard and had to wait months for their pay and rations, which were shipped to St. Augustine from Spain or Mexico and were always late in coming [Pickett and Pickett 2011, 93].

Perhaps the worst abuse facing the settlers was how they received their rations. The people were supported with cash, which they were to use to buy their food and goods from the governor. Of course, he charged exorbitant prices.

The fort really served as a frontier outpost with about 300 occupants. Many of the soldiers brought their wives with them, or married Amerindians, but the colony had to be supported by the Crown and did not generate profit. When Menéndez died, it was ruled by his heirs until 1576, at which point it became a Crown colony with a royally appointed governor. This was a model very different from the English and French colonial efforts, where their colonies were expected to generate a profit. For the French in Québec, that would be furs, and for the English in Jamestown, that would be tobacco.

Establishment of the Mission System

In the seventeenth century, the major settlement activity of the Spanish in La Florida became the establishment of missions. Because attracting colonists to Florida was difficult, "the authorities tried to compensate by transforming Indians into Hispanics through the agency of Franciscan Missionaries" (Taylor 2001, 78).

The authorities hoped that missions could consolidate control of the interior much more cheaply than sending soldiers. During the expansion of the Franciscan mission system between 1595 and through the 1620s, almost all the Timucua chiefdoms were incorporated into Spain's La Florida colony, as were the Guale Indians of the Georgia coast

(Milanich 2000). In the 1630s, the Apalachee Indians of eastern northwest Florida were also included in the mission system.

The maintenance of the vast mission system of Spain in La Florida would become a substantial drain on the treasury. However, "with converts counted in the thousands, the Spanish crown could not abandon the new Christians and the obligation to provide priests and necessities for Catholic worship and a Christian life" (Parker 2014, 561).

Life of the Missionaries

From 1632 to 1674, the great numerical increase in the number of Florida's baptized natives led the Catholic historian Maynard Geiger (1937) to call the period the "Golden Age" of the Florida missions. However, Spellman (1965, 355) suggested that the hardships suffered by the friars could hardly make it a Golden Age:

> The so-called "Golden Age" was a time of unrelieved poverty and hardship for the friars, of hunger and want and near-slavery for the Indians, of acrimonious disputes between missionaries and officials, of violent Indian revolts, and of equally violent civil suppressions.

Spellman (1965) also describes a letter that was sent from Fray Francisco Alonzo de Jesus, *custodio*—or superior—of the Franciscan Province of Santa Elena to the king in 1635. In it, he cries out for more priests and bemoans their short life expectancies. Among 12 priests that arrived in 1630, one died en route, two were too ill to leave Cuba, five died soon after arrival, and the remainder were mostly infirm and exhausted.

Another letter to the king written by Franciscan Fray Francisco Perez in 1646 outlined the discouraging paucity of missionaries everywhere in Florida and their great level of suffering. Forty-three Franciscans were working in the field at that date, but they were not even close to the numbers necessary to adequately meet the needs of the Indians.

Spellman (1965, 358) suggested that "the hardships experienced boggled the imagination." He described how Florida's mission system "was 150 leagues of swampy, mosquito-infested woodlands, where extremes of heat and cold and the frequent lack of food, clothing ... were the cause of mounting discouragement to the zeal and goodwill of the friars."

The lot of the Amerindians on the missions was also dire. They were forced to clear and work the fields with limited numbers of axes and hoes. They went naked and hungry. In bad crop years, they literally starved—no one escaped great suffering.

The Great Indigenous Societies Crash

As the seventeenth century progressed, the great Indigenous cultures of Florida essentially collapsed (Milanich 1995). The Timucua, Calusa, Apalachee, Tocobaga, and Ais people, who had long resisted Spanish incursions, finally succumbed to Spanish expeditions, raids by South Carolinian slavers and their Indigenous allies, and especially disease. Large parts of the peninsula were mostly vacant by the 1700s, and Creek immigrants began to arrive who had been chased off their land by the encroachment of South Carolinian settlements. These were joined by fleeing African slaves. These groups, along with the few Indigenous survivors, would join together to form what became the Seminoles.

The depopulation meant the end of the mission system. There were several new Spanish attempts at colonization, but they all failed due to ineffective leadership, disease, and hurricanes. The Spanish were gradually boxed in by the English Province of Carolina in 1639, French New Orleans in 1718, and Great Britain's Province of Georgia in 1732. Today's border of Florida was established in 1748 at the conclusion of the War of Jenkins' Ear or Anglo-Spanish War, fought mostly in the Caribbean but also including a Georgia Colony attack on St. Augustine and a failed invasion of Georgia by Spain.

Bibliography

Adler, J. 2020. "The History of the Verrazzano-Narrows Bridge, 50 Years After Its Construction." *Smithsonian Magazine*. https://www.smithsonianmag.com/history/history-verrazano-narrows-bridge-50-years-after-its-construction-180953032/.
Allender, M. 2018. "Glass Beads and Spanish Shipwrecks." *Historical Archaeology* 52(4): 824–43.
Altman, I. 2018. "The Spanish Caribbean, 1492–1550." *Oxford Research Encyclopedia of Latin American History*. https://doi.org/10.1093/acrefore/9780199366439.013.630.
Andrews, C.M., and E.W. Andrews. 1945. *Jonathan Dickinson's journal or God's protecting providence. Being the narrative of a journey from Port Royal in Jamaica to Philadelphia between August 23, 1696, to April 1, 1697*. Yale University Press.
Arnold, J.B., and M.A. Wickman. 2021. "Padre Island Spanish Shipwrecks of 1554." Texas State Historical Association. https://www.tshaonline.org/handbook/entries/padre-island-spanish-shipwrecks-of-1554.
Bandelier, F. 1905. *The Journey of Alvar Nuñez Cabeza de Vaca and His Companions from Florida to the Pacific, 1528–1536*. A.S. Barnes & Company.
Barlowe, A. 1880. *Old South Leaflets 92. The First Voyage Made to the Coasts of America, with Two Barks, wherein Were Captains M. Philip Amadas and M. Arthur Barlowe, Who Discovered Part of the Countrey now called Virginia, Anno 1584*. Academic Affairs Library, University of North Carolina. https://archive.org/details/firstvoyagetoroa00barl/page/n1/mode/2up.
Bernstein, W.J. 2008. *A Splendid Exchange: How Trade Shaped the World*. Grove Press.
Blitz, J.H. 2007. "Mississippian Period." *Encyclopedia of Alabama*. Alabama Humanities Foundation. https://encyclopediaofalabama.org/article/mississippian-period/.
Boucher, C.L.M. 2018. "The Greatest Dissemblers in the World: Timucuas, Spaniards, and the Fall of Fort Caroline." *The Florida Historical Quarterly* 97(2): 143–66.
Bourne, E.G., ed. 1904. *Narratives of the Career of Hernando de Soto in the Conquest of Florida, as told by a Knight of Elvas and in a Relation by Luys Hernandez de Biedma, Factor of the Expedition. Together with an Account of de Soto's Expedition Based on the Diary of Rodrigo Ranjel, His Private Secretary*. Translated by Buckingham Smith from Oviedo's *Historia General y Natural de las Indias*. Barnes and Company.
Burnett, G. 1986. *Florida's Past*, Vol. 1. Pineapple Press.
Burrage, H.S. 1906. *Early English and French Voyages: 1534–1608*. Charles Scribner's Sons.
Burrows, E.G., and M. Wallace. 1999. *Gotham: A History of New York City to 1898*. Oxford University Press.
Campbell, T.N. 1995. "Quevene Indians." Handbook of Texas Online. https://www.tshaonline.org/handbook/entries/quevene-indians.
Cartwright, G. 1998. *Galveston: A History of the Island*. Chisholm Trail Series, Volume18. TCU Press.
Cartwright, M. 2020. "The Sea Dogs—Queen Elizabeth's Privateers." *World History*

Bibliography

Encyclopedia. https://www.worldhistory.org/article/1576/the-sea-dogs---queen-elizabeths-privateers/.
Chapman, R. 2015. "Throwing the Explorer Out with the Fountain: American History Textbooks and Juan Ponce de León." *Florida Historical Quarterly* 94(1): 92–108.
"Charter to Sir Walter Raleigh: 1584." 2022. The Avalon Project. Yale Law School, Lillian Goldman Law Library. https://avalon.law.yale.edu/16th_century/raleigh.asp.
Clayton, L.A., E.C. Moore, and V.J. Knight. 1995. *The De Soto Chronicles: The Expedition of Hernando de Soto to North America in 1539–1543.* University of Alabama Press.
Codignola, L. 1999. "Another Look at Verrazzano's Voyage, 1524." *Journal of the History of the Atlantic Region* 29(1): 29–42.
Cogswell, J.G., trans. 1841. *The Voyage of John de Verrazzano, Along the Coast of North America, from Carolina to Newfoundland, A.D. 1524.* Collections of the New York Historical Society, Second series, Volume 1, 37–67.
Davenport, H., ed. 1923. "The Expedition of Pánfilo de Narváez by Gonzalo Fernández Oviedo y Valdes." *The Southwestern Historical Quarterly* 27(2): 120–39.
Davidson, R.I. 2004. *Indian River: A History of the Ais Indians in Spanish Florida.* Ais Indian Project Publication. Publication of Archival Library & Museum Materials, State University Libraries of Florida.
Davis, T.F. 1935. "History of Juan Ponce de León's Voyages to Florida: Source Records." Document No. AJ-095. Wisconsin Historical Society, Digital Library and Archives. https://content.wisconsinhistory.org/digital/collection/aj/id/12071.
"De Soto Trail: National historic trail study final report." 1990. National Park Service Southeast Regional Office. http://npshistory.com/publications/transportation/desoto-nht.pdf.
Deagan, K. 1978. "The Material Assemblage of 16th-Century Spanish Florida." *Historical Archaeology* 12: 31–50.
DePratter, C.B. 1991. *Late Prehistoric and Early Historic Chiefdoms in the Southeastern United States.* Garland.
DePratter, C.B., C.M. Hudson, and M.T. Smith. 1983. "The Route of Juan Pardo's Explorations in the Interior Southeast, 1566–1568." *Florida Historical Quarterly* 62(2): 125–58.
Drolet, R., and R. Stryker. n.d. "Spanish Shipwrecks in 1554: 'The Wreck of the 300.'" Corpus Christi Museum of Science and History. https://www.texasbeyondhistory.net/coast/images/he4.html.
Durand-Gasselin, T. n.d. "Huguenot Pirates in the 16th Century." Musée protestant. https://museeprotestant.org/en/notice/huguenot-pirates-in-the-17th-century/.
Evans, P.W. 2006. "Amadas and Barlowe Expedition." *Encyclopedia of North Carolina.* University of North Carolina Press. https://www.ncpedia.org/amadas-and-barlowe-expedition.
Geake, R.A. 2011. *A History of the Narragansett Nation of Rhode Island.* The History Press.
Geiger, M.J. 1937. *The Franciscan Conquest of Florida (1573–1618).* Catholic University of America.
Greenspan, J. 2013. "The Myth of Ponce de León and the Fountain of Youth." *History.* https://www.history.com/news/the-myth-of-ponce-de-leon-and-the-fountain-of-youth.
Hakluyt, R. 1904. *The Principal Navigations Voyages Traffiques and Discoveries of the English Nation,* Vol. 8. Macmillan Company.
Hancock, J.F. 2022. "The Iberian Conquest of the Americas." *World History Encyclopedia.* https://www.worldhistory.org/article/1920/the-iberian-conquest-of-the-americas/.
Hann, J.H. 2003. *Indians of Central and South Florida 1513–1763.* University Press of Florida.
Harriot, T. 1590. *A Briefe and True Report of the New Found Land of Virginia: of the*

Bibliography

Commodities and of the Nature and Manners of the Naturall Inhabitants. https://archive.org/details/briefetruereport00harr.

Harris, S. 1963. "The Tragic Dream of Jean Ribaut." *American Heritage* 14(16). https://www.americanheritage.com/tragic-dream-jean-ribaut.

"Hernando de Soto." 2023. National Park Service. National Historical Park Georgia, Ocmulgee Mounds. https://www.nps.gov/ocmu/learn/historyculture/hernando-desoto.htm.

Hirst, K. 2021. "Mississippians Were the Mound Builders in North America." ThoughtCo. https://www.thoughtco.com/mississippian-culture-moundbuilder-171721.

Hoffman, B.G. 1961. *Cabot to Cartier: Sources for a Historical Ethnography of Northeastern North America 1497–1550.* The University of Toronto Press.

Hoffman, P.E. 1980. "A New Voyage of North American Discovery: Pedro de Salazar's Visit to the 'Island of Giants.'" *The Florida Historical Quarterly* 58(4): 415–26.

Hoffman, P.E. 1983. "Legend, Religious Idealism, and Colonies: The Point of Santa Elena in History, 1552–1566." *The South Carolina Historical Magazine* 84(2): 59–71.

Hoffman, P.E. 1984. "The Chicora Legend and Franco-Spanish Rivalry in La Florida." *The Florida Historical Quarterly* 62(4): 419–38.

Hoffman, P.E. 1990. *A New Andalucia and a Way to the Orient: The American Southeast During the Sixteenth Century.* Louisiana State University Press.

Holloway, M. 2016. "Uncovering the Luna Colony, a Lost Remnant of Spanish Florida." *New Yorker.* https://www.newyorker.com/news/news-desk/uncovering-the-luna-colony-a-lost-remnant-of-spanish-florida.

Hudson, C. 1976. *The Southeastern Indians.* University of Tennessee Press.

Hudson, C. 1988. "A Spanish-Coosa Alliance in Sixteenth-Century North Georgia." *The Georgia Historical Quarterly* 72(4): 599–626.

Hudson, C. 1997. *Knights of Spain, Warriors of the Sun: Hernando de Soto and the South's Ancient Chiefdoms.* University of Georgia Press.

Hudson, C., M. Smith, D. Hally, R. Polhemus, and C. DePratter. 1985. "Coosa: A Chiefdom in the Sixteenth-Century Southeastern United States." *American Antiquity* 50(4): 723–37.

Hudson, C., M.T. Smith, C.B. DePratter, and E. Kelly. 1989. "The Tristán de Luna Expedition, 1559–1561." *Southeastern Archaeology* 8(1): 31–45.

"Huguenots." 2022. *History.* https://www.history.com/topics/european-history/huguenots.

Hurt, R.D. 1987. *Indian Agriculture in America: Prehistory to Present.* University of Kansas Press.

Jarus, O. 2021. "What Happened to the 'Vanished' Colonists at Roanoke?" LiveScience. https://www.livescience.com/vanished-colonists-at-roanoke.

Johnson, J.G. 1923. "A Spanish Settlement in Carolina, 1526." *The Georgia Historical Quarterly* 7(4): 339–45.

Jones, G.D. 1978. "The Ethnohistory of the Guale Coast through 1684." In *The Anthropology of St. Catherines Island 1: Natural and Cultural History, Anthropological Papers*, Volume 55, part 2, edited by D.H. Thomas, G.D. Jones, and R.S. Durham. American Museum of Natural History.

Koch, A., C. Brierley, M.M. Maslin, and S.L. Lewis. 2019. "Earth System Impacts of the European Arrival and Great Dying in the Americas after 1492." *Quaternary Science Reviews* 207: 13–36.

Lamarche, S.R. 2019. *Tainos and Caribs: The Aboriginal Cultures of the Antilles.* Editorial Punto y Coma.

Larkin, R. 2016. "Journey Through Time: Commemorating the 450th Anniversary of Juan Pardo's Exploration of the Carolinas." *WNC Magazine.* https://wncmagazine.com/feature/journey_through_time.

Laudonnière, R. 1975. *Three Voyages.* Translated by C.E. Bennett. University Presses of Florida.

Bibliography

Lawler, A. 2018. "Did Francis Drake Bring Enslaved Africans to North America Decades Before Jamestown?" *Smithsonian Magazine*. https://www.smithsonianmag.com/history/did-francis-drake-bring-enslaved-africans-north-america-decades-jamestown-180970075/.

Lipscomb, C.A., and T. Seiter. 1976. "Karankawa Indians." Handbook of Texas Online. Published by the Texas State Historical Association. https://www.tshaonline.org/handbook/entries/karankawa-indians.

Lowery, M.M. 2018. *The Lumbee Indians: An American Struggle*. The University of North Carolina Press.

Lowery, W. 1911. *The Spanish Settlements Within the Present Limits of the United States: Florida, 1562–1574*. G.P. Putnam's Sons.

Lyon, E. 1976. *The Enterprise of Florida: Pedro Menéndez de Avilés and the Spanish Conquest of 1565–1568*. University Presses of Florida.

Lyon, E. 1984. "Santa Elena: A Brief History of the Colony, 1566–1587." Archaeology and Anthropology Research Manuscript Series, University of South Carolina, Scholar Commons.

Lyon, E. 1988. "Pedro Menéndez's Strategic Plan for the Florida Peninsula." *The Florida Historical Quarterly* 67(1): 1–14.

Marquardt, W.R. 2004. "Calusa." In *Handbook of North American Indians, Vol. 14: Southeast*, edited by R.D. Fogelson. Smithsonian Institution.

Martínez-Fernández, L. 2015. "Far Beyond the Line: Corsairs, Privateers and Invading Settlers in Cuba and the Caribbean (1529–1670)." *Revista de Indias* 75(263): 7–38.

McCartney, M.W. 2005. "Chapter 4: Narrative History." In *A Study of Virginia Indians and Jamestown*, principal investigator D. Moretti-Langholtz. Colonial National Historical Park, National Park Service, U.S. Department of the Interior Cooperative Agreement # CA 4290-0-0001. https://www.nps.gov/parkhistory/online_books/jame1/moretti-langholtz/chap4.htm.

McEwan, B.G. 2004. "Apalachee and Neighboring Groups." In *Handbook of North American Indians, Vol. 14: Southeast*, edited by R.D. Fogelson. Smithsonian Institution.

McGrath, J. 1997. "A Massacre Revised: Matanzas, 1565." In *Proceedings of the Meeting of the French Colonial Historical Society, Vol. 21: Essays in French Colonial History*. Michigan State University Press.

Milanich, J.T. 1989. "Where Did de Soto Land? Identifying Bahia Honda." *The Florida Anthropologist* 42(4): 295–302.

Milanich, J.T. 1995. *Florida Indians and the Invasion from Europe*. University Press of Florida.

Milanich, J.T. 1996. *The Timucua*. Blackwell Publications.

Milanich, J.T. 2000. "The Timucua Indians of Northern Florida and Southern Georgia." In *Indians of the Greater Southeast: Historical Archaeology and Ethnohistory*, edited by B.G. McEwan. University Press of Florida.

Minster, C. 2020. "Explorer Pánfilo de Narváez Found Disaster in Florida." ThoughtCo. https://www.thoughtco.com/biography-of-panfilo-de-narvaez-2136335.

Moore, P.N. 2019. "Indigenous Power and Collapse on the Lower South Carolina Coast, Precontact–1684." *The South Carolina Historical Magazine* 120(1): 4–29.

Morison, S.L. 1971. *The European Discovery of America. The Northern Voyages. A.D. 500–1600*. Oxford University Press.

"Native Americans of the South Outer Banks." 2015. National Park Service. Cape Lookout, National Seashore, North Carolina. https://www.nps.gov/calo/learn/historyculture/nativeamericans.htm.

Newcomb, W.W. 2010. *The Indians of Texas: From Prehistoric to Modern Times*. University of Texas Press.

Oberg, M.L. 2007. *The Head in Edward Nugent's Hand: Roanoke's Forgotten Indians*. University of Pennsylvania Press.

Bibliography

Ortiz, A., ed. 1978. *Southwest.* Handbook of North American Indians, vol. 10. Smithsonian Institution.
Paravisini-Gebert, L. 2016. "Food, Biodiversity, Extinctions: Caribbean Fauna and the Struggle for Food Security During the Conquest of the New World." *Journal of West Indian Literature* 24(2): 11–26.
Parker, S.R. 2014. "St. Augustine in the Seventeenth-Century: Capital of La Florida." *The Florida Historical Quarterly* 92(3): 554–76.
Parks, G.B. 1890. *Richard Hakluyt and the English Voyages.* American Geographical Society, New York. https://archive.org/details/richardhakluyten0000park.
Peck, D.T. 2001. "Lucas Vásquez de Ayllón's Doomed Colony of San Miguel de Gualdape." *The Georgia Historical Quarterly* 85(2): 183–98.
Perkins, F.B. 1875. *Narrative of Le Moyne, an Artist Who Accompanied the French Expedition to Florida Under Laudonnière, 1564.* J.R. Osgood and Company.
Pickett, M.F., and D.W. Pickett. 2011. *The European Struggle to Settle North America: Colonizing Attempts by England, France, and Spain, 1521–1608.* McFarland.
Priestley, H.I. 1928. *The Luna Papers: Documents Relating to the Expedition of Don Tristán de Luna y Arellano for the Conquest of La Florida in 1559–1561.* De Land: Florida State Historical Society.
Prins, H.E.L., and B. McBride. 2007. *Asticou's Island Domain: Wabanaki Peoples at Mount Desert Island 1500–2000.* Ethnography Program Northeast Region, National Park Service, U.S. Department of the Interior.
Probasco, N. 2017. "Catherine de Medici and Huguenot Colonization, 1560–1567." In *Colonization, Piracy, and Trade in Early Modern Europe: Queenship and Power,* edited by E. Paranque, N. Probasco, and C. Jowitt. Palgrave Macmillan.
Quattlebaum, P. 1956. *The Land Called Chicora: The Carolinas Under Spanish Rule with French Intrusions, 1520–1670.* University of Florida Press.
Quinn, D.B. 1974. *England and the Discovery of America, 1481–1620: From the Bristol Voyages of the Fifteenth Century to the Pilgrim Settlement at Plymouth: The Exploration, Exploitation, and Trial-and-Error Colonization of North America by the English.* A.A. Knopf.
Reilly, S.E. 1981. "A Marriage of Expedience: The Calusa Indians and Their Relations with Pedro Menéndez de Avilés in Southwest Florida, 1566–1569." *The Florida Historical Quarterly* 59(4): 395–421.
Ribault, Jean. 1927. *The Whole & True Discouerye of Terra Florida: A Facsimile Reprint of the London Edition of 1563, Together with a Transcript of an English Version in the British Museum.* Translated by J.T. Connor. Publications of the Florida Historical Society.
Ricky, D. 2001. *The Encyclopedia of Georgia Indians: Indians of Georgia and the Southeast.* Somerset Publishers, Inc.
Ricky, D.B. 1998. *The Encyclopedia of Florida Indians: Tribes, Nations and People of the Woodland Area.* Somerset Publishers, Inc.
Ross, M. 1923. "French Intrusions and Indian Uprisings in Georgia and South Carolina (1577–1580)." *The Georgia Historical Quarterly* 7(3): 251–81.
Rudes, B.A. 2004. *Pre-Columbian Links to the Caribbean: Evidence Connecting Cusabo to Taino.* Language Variety in the South III Conference, Tuscaloosa, AL.
Sabo, G., III. 2023. "Native Americans." *Encyclopedia of Arkansas.* Central Arkansas Library System. https://encyclopediaofarkansas.net/entries/Native-Americans-408/.
Sandler, M.W. 2008. *Atlantic Ocean: The Illustrated History of the Ocean that Changed the World.* Sterling.
Sauer, C.O. 1971. *Sixteenth Century North America: The Land and Its People as Seen by the Europeans.* University of California Press.
Saunders, R. 2000. "The Guale Indians of the Lower Atlantic Coast: Change and Continuity." In *Indians of the Greater Southeast: Historical Archaeology and Ethnohistory,* edited by B.G. McEwan. University Press of Florida.

Bibliography

Simmonds, W.S. 1989. *The Narragansett*. Chelsea House Publishers.
Smith, M. 2019. "Late Prehistoric/Early Historic Chiefdoms." *New Georgia Encyclopedia*. https://www.georgiaencyclopedia.org/articles/history-archaeology/late-prehistoric-early-historic-chiefdoms-ca-a-d-1300-1850/.
Solís de Merás, G. 2017. *Pedro Menéndez de Avilés and the Conquest of Florida: A New Manuscript*. Edited, translated, and annotated by D. Arbesú. University Press of Florida.
Spellman, C.W. 1965. "The 'Golden Age' of the Florida Missions, 1632–1674." *The Catholic Historical Review* 51(3): 354–72.
Stone, E.W. 2014. "Indian Harvest: The Rise of the Indigenous Slave Trade and Diaspora from Española to the Circum-Caribbean, 1492–1542." PhD diss., Vanderbilt University.
Sturtevant, W.C. 1961. "Taino Agriculture." In *The Evolution of Horticultural Systems in Native South America, Causes and Consequences: A Symposium*, edited by J. Wilbert. Sociedad de Ciencias Naturales La Salle, Caracas.
Swanton, J.R. 1922. *Early History of the Creek Indians and Their Neighbors*. Washington Government Printing Office.
Taylor, A. 2001. *American Colonies: The Settling of North America*. Penguin Books.
Thornton 2014. "The Calusa People." AccessGeneology.com. https://accessgenealogy.com/florida/calusa-people.htm.
"Timucuan: Original Florida Natives." 2018. Castillo de San Marcos, National Monument Florida, National Park Service. https://www.nps.gov/casa/learn/historyculture/timucua.htm.
Turner, S. 2013. "Juan Ponce de León and the Discovery of Florida Reconsidered." *Florida Historical Quarterly* 92(1): 1–31.
Vigneras, L.A. 1969. "A Spanish Discovery of North Carolina in 1566." *The North Carolina Historical Review* 46(4): 398–414.
Waddell, G. 1980. *Indians of the South Carolina Lowcountry, 1562–1751*. Southern Studies Program, University of South Carolina.
Waddell, G. 2005. "Cofitachequi: A Distinctive Culture, Its Identity, and Its Location." *Ethnohistory* 52(2): 333–69.
Weddle, R.S. 1985. *Spanish Sea: The Gulf of Mexico in North American Discovery, 1500–1685*. Texas A&M University Press.
Weisert, K. 2021. "Timucua Tribe—Lost Today." Legends of America. Temucuan Ecological and Historic Preserve. Jacksonville, Florida. https://www.legendsofamerica.com/fl-timucuatribe/.
Wenhold, L.L. 1956. "Manrique de Rojas' Report on French Settlement in Florida, 1564." *The Florida Historical Quarterly* 38: 45–62.
Weslager, C.A. 1972. *The Delaware Indians: A History*. Rutgers University Press.
Wolfe, B. 2021. "Don Luís de Velasco / Paquiquineo (fl. 1561–1571)." *Encyclopedia Virginia*. https://encyclopediavirginia.org/entries/don-luis-de-velasco-paquiquineo-fl-1561-1571/.
Wolfe, B. 2022. "Roanoke Colonies." *Encyclopedia Virginia*. https://encyclopediavirginia.org/entries/roanoke-colonies-the.
Worth, J.E. 1995. "Fontaneda Revisited: Five Descriptions of Sixteenth-Century Florida." *The Florida Historical Quarterly* 73(3): 339–52.
Worth, J.E. 2014. *Discovering Florida: First Contact Narratives from Spanish Expeditions Along the Lower Gulf Coast*. University Press of Florida.
Wroth, L.C. 1970. *The Voyages of Giovanni da Verrazzano, 1524–1528*. Yale University Press.

Index

Ais 16, 22, 122, 128, 129, 145, 169, 175
Ajacán 127, 144, 145
Algonquian 42, 49, 157, 158, 159, 160, 165
Alvarado, García de Escalante 84
Alvarado, Luis de Moscoso 77
Amadas, Philip 153, 155, 156, 159, 160
Anilco 77, 81
Apalachee: location 57, 58, 86, 149; people 9, 10, 55, 57, 63, 64, 69, 70, 81, 174, 175
Arcadia 42, 44
Armada de la Carrera 116
Aquixo 75, 81

Barlowe, Arthur 153, 154, 155, 156, 157, 159
Beniny 14, 19
Bobadilla, Francisco 6, 68

Calusa 9, 10, 17, 21, 22, 81, 123, 133, 138, 139, 169, 175
Caravallo 57
Caribs 19, 20
Carlos 68, 123, 124, 125, 126, 127, 128, 133, 136, 137, 138, 139, 170
Casqui 76, 77
Catawba 10, 35
Cathay 43, 47
Cèllere Codex 40
Cerón, Juan 14
Charlesfort 101, 102, 103, 107, 130, 170
Chickasaw 10, 35, 74, 81
Chicora 27, 29, 30, 31, 35, 85, 97, 171
Cherokee 10
Chiaha 73, 35
Chisca 134, 135
Choctaw 10
Cofitachequi 72, 81, 82, 134
Columbus, Christopher 5, 6, 7, 10, 13, 38, 39

Columbus, Diego 14, 18, 29
Coosa: location 89, 90, 90, 95, 170; people 9, 74, 81, 86, 88, 89, 90, 91, 92, 93, 94, 135
Coree 42, 49
Cortés, Hernán 8, 20, 48, 54
Creek 10, 135
Croatoan 157, 159, 164, 165, 166
Cusabo 9, 35, 143

Da Gama, Vasco 39
Dare, Virginia 164
Dasemunkepeuc 155, 161, 163, 164
da Verrazzano, Giovanni 38, 40, 41, 42, 43, 44, 45, 46, 47, 48, 49, 50, 51, 85, 159, 169
da Verrazzano, Girolamo 41
Dávila, Pedrarias "the Cruel" 68, 70, 86
de Amaya, Diego 123
de Arciniega, Sancho 132
de Ayllón, Lucas Vázquez 27, 28, 29, 30, 31, 32, 33, 34, 35, 53, 72, 169, 171
de Cáncer, Luis 80
de Canço, Gonzalo Méndez 172
de Châtillon, Gaspard Coligny 97, 170
de Chicora, Francisco 29, 31, 32, 33, 72
de Cos, García Martínez 138
Dee, John 151
de Esquivel, Juan 7
de Luna, Tristán 81, 85, 86, 87, 88, 93, 94, 95, 127, 135, 169, 170, 171
de Medrano, Juan Vélez 122
de Oviedo, Lope 61, 62
de Gourgues, Dominique 141, 142, 143
de Guzmán, Pedro Núñez 13
de Herrera, Antonio 15, 16, 17, 18
de Jesus, Fray Francisco Alonzo 174
de la Anunciación, Domingo 86, 88, 89, 91, 92
de las Alas, Estaban 129, 130, 131

183

Index

de Laudonnière, René Goulaine 100, 101, 102, 103, 104, 105, 106, 107, 108, 109, 110, 119, 170, 171
del Castillo, Alonso 62
de León, Juan Ponce 7, 8, 13, 63, 80, 81, 115, 124, 169
del Sauz, Mateo 88, 89, 92, 93, 94, 95
de Merás, Solís 118, 125, 126, 138
de Morales, Hernando Moyano 134, 135
de Narváez, Pánfilo 53, 54, 55, 56, 57, 58, 59, 61, 63, 69, 70, 80, 81, 85, 115, 169
de Olmos, Alonso 144
de Ovando, Frey Nicolás 6, 7
de Oviedo, Gonzalo Fernández 20, 22, 30, 53, 54, 67
de Quejo, Pedro 28, 29, 31, 32
de Reynoso, Francisco 133, 137, 139
de Salazar, Domingo 88
de Salazar, Pedro 20, 27, 28, 33, 169, 171
de Soro, Hernando Mendez 66, 68, 69, 85, 89; in Alabama 73; in Arkansas and Great Plains 76; death 77; in Georgia 71; legacy 79; in Mississippi 75; people met 81; in South Carolina 72
de Vaca, Álvar Núñez Cabeza 53, 56, 57, 58, 59, 61, 62, 63, 65, 170
de Valdés, Pedro 129
de Velasco, Luis 85, 127, 146
de Villafañe, Ángel 84, 95, 127
de Villarroel, Gonzalo 139
Dominicans 33, 80, 127, 145
Doña Antonia 126, 127, 129, 133, 136, 138
Doncel, Gines 34
Don Felipe 127, 131, 136, 139
Dorantes, Andrés 62
Drake, Francis Sir 148, 151, 152, 159, 162

Elizabeth 101, 151, 152, 153, 171
Estevanico 62

Ferdinand II 14, 19, 20, 21
Fontaneda, Hernando de Escalante 124
Fort Caroline 104, 106, 110, 119, 120, 142
Fort San Felipe 144, 145, 146
Fort San Juan 135
Fort San Pedro 135
Fort Santiago 136
Fort Santo Tomás 136
Fountain of Youth 21
Franciscan missionaries 149, 173, 174, 182

Gambié, Pierre 106
Gilbert, Sir Humphrey 152

Gómez, Captain Fransisco 34, 35
Gordillo, Francisco 28, 29, 33
Grajales, Father Francisco López de Mendoza 119
Granganimeo 155, 160, 161
Great Dying 10, 102
Grenville, Sir Richard 158, 159, 160, 162
Guacanagari 5
Guale 9, 34, 100, 103, 111, 130, 131, 144, 145, 146, 147, 148, 170, 173

Hakluyt, Richard 151, 152
Harriot, Thomas 153, 157, 158, 166
Hawkins, John 109, 110, 151
Hispaniola 5, 6, 7, 13, 14, 17, 27, 29, 30, 35, 38, 54, 80, 95
Historia general y natural de las Indias 20, 30, 54, 67
Howe, George 163
Hudson, Henry 48
Huguenots 96, 97, 101, 103, 115, 120, 170
Huhasene 78, 81

Inca 8, 68
Isabella, Queen 6, 7, 8

Jesuit 127, 136, 143, 144, 149

Karankawa 60, 65, 84
King's Patent 14

La Dauphine 41
Lady of Cofitachequi 71
La Isabela 5
La Navidad 5
Land called Chicora 29, 169
Le Challeux, Nicolas 97, 117, 119
Legend of Chicora 27, 30, 72
Le Moyne, Jaquez 97, 98, 103, 104, 105, 106, 107, 108, 109, 110, 117, 119
Lenni Lenape 50
Lost Colony 162

Mabila 73, 74, 87, 88
Magellan, Ferdinand 48
Manteo 156, 157, 159, 160, 161, 162, 163, 164, 165
Márquez, Pedro Menéndez 136, 139, 147, 148, 149
Martyr, Peter 31
Menatonon 160, 161
Menéndez, Pedro: activities first year 121, 122, 123; another attempt to settle Ajacán 14, 144, 145; back to Spain

Index

141; Calusa visits 123, 124, 125, 126, 127; commission and background 115, 116; 117; establishes Santa Elena 130, 131; first expedition 116, 117, 118, 119; last visit to Florida 145; makes Santa Elena capitol 143; mission to Ajacán 127; relief of Florida 123; relocates St. Augustine 132; return to land of Carlos 136, 137; returns east 139, 140; reunites with wife 133; struggles to control Florida 128, 129
Mission system 173
Mound Key 24, 124, 138

Nanipacana 88, 88
Napochi 92, 94, 95
Narragansett 45
Narragansett (people) 45, 46, 51
New York 44, 48, 50, 169
Nugent, Edward 161

Ochuse 85, 86, 170
Orista 35, 136, 143, 144, 146, 147, 148
Ortiz, Juan 70, 71, 77, 156, 159
Ossomocomuck 155

Pacaha 75, 76, 77, 81
Padre Island shipwrecks 83
Pamlico Sound 42, 43, 47, 159
Pardo, Juan 81, 131, 134, 135
Pemisapan 161, 162
Perez, Fray Francisco 174
Philip II 85, 103, 111, 121, 127, 143, 146, 147, 149
Piachi 87, 88
Pizarro, Francisco 8, 68
Polonza 87, 88, 94, 95, 127
Port Royal 33, 35, 101, 104, 147

Raleigh, Sir Walter 41, 151, 152, 153, 157, 158, 162, 163, 171
Ramirez, Juan 34
Ranjel, Rodrigo 67, 70, 72, 73, 74, 75, 76, 77
Ribault, Jean 96, 97; first visit and colony 98, 99, 100, 101, 102, 103, 104, 110, 111; return and massacre by Spanish 110, 119
Roanoke: colony 148, 162, 163, 164, 165;

people 9, 42, 49, 155, 156, 157, 161, 164, 165; place 13, 42, 154, 155, 156, 157, 160, 161, 165
Rogel, Father Juan 136, 138, 139, 143, 144, 149

Safety Harbor Culture 55, 63, 68, 81
St. Augustine 13, 22, 33, 98, 118, 119, 121, 123, 129, 131, 132, 133, 137, 141, 142, 145, 146, 147, 148, 149, 150, 158, 162, 170, 172, 173, 175
San Cristobal 15, 16, 19
San Felipe 131, 134, 141, 144, 145, 146
San Mateo 88, 121, 123, 127, 128, 129, 137, 139, 141, 142, 143, 158
San Miguel de Gualdape 34, 171
Santa Elena 85, 86, 95, 127, 130, 131, 134, 135, 136, 143, 144, 145, 146, 148, 149, 170, 171, 174
Santa Lucia 128
Santa Maria 5
Santa Maria de la Consolación 15, 19
Santa Maria de San Vicente 160
Saturiwa 104, 105, 111, 139, 140, 142
Secotan 154, 155, 157, 166
Shakori 27, 28, 29, 35
Shawnee 35
Skiko 161, 162

Tacatacuru 111, 142
Taíno 5, 6, 7, 8, 13, 16, 21, 27
Timucua 9, 10, 63, 81, 99, 105, 106, 107, 108, 111, 118, 119, 120, 121, 122, 132, 142, 170, 173, 175
Tocobaga 55, 63, 80, 137, 138, 139, 175
Tuscaloosa 3, 74, 81

Utina 105, 107, 111
Uzita 63, 768, 0, 81

Velázquez, Diego 7, 54
Vélez, Juan 122, 123
Verrazzano Narrows Bridge 44

Wabanaki 47
Wanchese 157, 158, 160, 162
White, John 42, 153, 158, 160, 163, 164, 165, 166
Wingina 155, 156, 157, 159, 161

www.ingramcontent.com/pod-product-compliance
Lightning Source LLC
Chambersburg PA
CBHW032047300426
44117CB00009B/1217